HOME COOKING

HOME COOKING

LAURIE COLWIN

Illustrated by Anna Shapiro

BANTAM BOOKS
NEW YORK · TORONTO · LONDON · SYDNEY · AUCKLAND

*This edition contains the complete text
of the original hardcover edition.*
NOT ONE WORD HAS BEEN OMITTED.

HOME COOKING

A Bantam Book / published by arrangement with Alfred A. Knopf, Inc.

*PRINTING HISTORY
Knopf edition published September 1988
Bantam edition / February 1990*

Portions of this text were originally published in *Gourmet*
magazine, *Inside* magazine, and *7 Days* magazine.

Library of Congress Cataloging-in-Publication Data
Colwin, Laurie.
    Home cooking / Laurie Colwin; illustrated by Anna Shapiro.
        p.   cm.
    Reprint. Originally published: New York : Knopf, 1988.
    ISBN 0-553-34807-8
    1. Cookery.   I. Title.
TX652.C714   1990
641.5—dc20   89-18116
                                                            CIP

Published simultaneously in the United States and Canada

PRINTED IN THE UNITED STATES OF AMERICA

CWO   0 9 8 7 6 5 4 3 2 1

To my sister, Leslie Friedman
(a great cook),
and to Juris and Rosa
(great eaters)

This edition
dedicated to the
Memory of Bill Whitehead,
colleague and friend

CONTENTS

FOREWORD

U nless you live alone in a cave or hermitage, cooking and eating are social activities: even hermit monks have one communal meal a month. The sharing of food is the basis of social life, and to many people it is the only kind of social life worth participating in.

No one who cooks cooks alone. Even at her most solitary, a cook in the kitchen is surrounded by generations of cooks past, the advice and menus of cooks present, the wisdom of cookbook writers. In my kitchen I rely on Edna Lewis, Marcella Hazan, Jane Grigson, Elizabeth David, the numerous contributors to *The Charleston Receipts*, and Margaret Costa (author of an English book entitled *The Four Seasons Cookery Book*).

One of the delights of life is eating with friends; second to that is *talking* about eating. And, for an unsurpassed double whammy, there is talking about eating *while* you are eating with friends. People who like to cook like to talk about food. Plain old cooks (as opposed to the geniuses in fancy restaurants) tend to be friendly. After all, without one cook giving another cook a tip or two, human life might have died out a long time ago.

For their inspiration and companionship, past and present, I would like to thank the following people with and for whom I have cooked, who have fed me delicious meals, and with whom I have talked endlessly about cooking, and whose recipes and menus I have shamelessly cribbed all these years.

Ann Arensberg, the ultimate home cook and menu planner without peer; Juliet Annan, a brilliant and fearless cook who knows that next to eating, the best thing is talking about eating; Frances Taliaferro whose every meal includes the major food groups plus brownies; Jeannette Kossuth who blends new age with Old Hungarian; Linda Faulhaber, a secret cook and great eater; Jeannie Heifetz, a bold experimenter, and Cinda Graham, both of whom will test-drive a recipe for a pal; Rob Wynne, artist and food genius whose meals are like birthday parties; Bonnie Maslin who proves that it is possible to be a great kosher cook; Willa Gelber and Rennis Garner, two generous caterers who share recipes; Alice Quinn who unites the elegant with the old-fashioned and will always make a popover for a friend; Carole Shookoff, friend, grammarian and cook; and my mother-in-law, Elza Jurjevics, a peerless baker. And, most of all, my mother, Estelle Colwin Snellenberg, who taught me and my sister all we know about good food, and how to make it look beautiful.

Thanks to Judith Jones, the true godmother of this book; Gail Zweigenthal of *Gourmet* magazine; Jane Biberman of *Inside* magazine; Liz Logan of *7 Days*; and last of all, to Victoria Wilson, the Escoffier of editors.

HOME COOKING:
AN INTRODUCTION

Unlike some people, who love to go out, I love to stay home. This may be caused by laziness, anxiety or xenophobia, and in the days when my friends were happily traveling to Bolivia and Nepal, I was ashamed to admit that what I liked best was hanging around the house.

I am probably not much fun as a traveler, either. My idea of a good time abroad is to visit someone's house and hang out, poking into their cupboards if they will let me. One summer I spent some time in a farmhouse on the island of Minorca. This was my idea of bliss: a vacation at home (even if it wasn't *my* home). I could wake up in the morning, make the coffee and wander outside to pick apricots for breakfast. I could wander around the markets figuring out that night's dinner. In foreign countries I am drawn into grocery shops, supermarkets and kitchen supply houses. I explain this by reminding my friends that, as I was taught in Introduction to Anthropology, it is not just the Great Works of mankind that make a culture. It is the daily things, like what people eat and how they serve it.

I love to eat out, but even more, I love to eat in. The best

dinner party I ever went to was a black-tie affair to celebrate a
book, catered by the author's sister. When we sat down in our
long dresses and tuxedos, my heart failed. What sort of fancy
something or other were we going to get? I remembered the sad
story told to me by a colleague who went to a white-tie dinner
and received, for the main course, one half of a flounder fillet.

When the food appeared at this party I could scarcely contain
my delight. It was home food! The most delicious kind: a savory
beef stew with olives and buttered noodles, a plain green salad
with a wonderful dressing, and some runny cheese and chocolate mousse for dessert. Heaven!

When people enter the kitchen, they often drag their childhood
in with them. I was brought up on English children's books, in
which teatime and cottage life play an important role. These
formed my earliest idea of comfort: a tea table in a cozy cottage.
As an adult I have reinforced these childhood notions by reading English cookbooks as if they were novels and rereading
such classics as *Consuming Passions* by Philippa Pullar, *An
Englishman's Food* by Drummond and Wilbraham, as well as
Food in England and *Lost Country Life* by Dorothy Hartley.

The thing about homebodies is that they can usually be found
at home. I usually am, and I like to feed people. Since I am a
writer by profession, it was inevitable that I would be inclined to
write about food. Now that these essays have been collected
into a book I feel it is only fair to explain a few biases.

This book abounds in recipes for chicken. Nowadays, almost
everyone I know has either given up red meat or restricts it
severely. Furthermore, I began to cook for myself at a time when
beef prices skyrocketed and people on tiny salaries simply ceased
to think about it. But chicken was and still is cheap.

I myself prefer an organic chicken. They are not easy to find,
but they are worth looking for. Organic eggs from free-range
chickens really and truly do taste better than anything you will
find in the supermarket. These are available at health food
stores and farmers' markets. These days most people have cut

down on eggs, but the few eggs you do eat ought to taste like eggs. As far as meat is concerned, if you have a source for organic beef or veal, go for it. Not only is it tastier (and frequently leaner), but you also do not have to worry about feeding anabolic steroids to friends and loved ones.

It is a depressing fact of life that we must now be so vigilant about what we eat. Not a day goes by that we are not told that something else is bad for us: butter, coffee, chocolate, tap water, wheat. When my daughter was a toddler and beginning to drink large quantities of apple juice, I (and the rest of the mothers in this country) learned that the apple crop was universally sprayed, year after year, with a known carcinogen and mutagen. Thereafter I began to order apple juice by the case from Walnut Acres, an organic farm in Penns Creek, Pennsylvania. I also routinely order organic applesauce, preservative-free yeast, and a remarkable organic bread flour. I have also invested in a high-tech water filter that removes just about everything (including fluoride—but this is not much of a problem since most children will eat toothpaste as if it were candy) from your water and makes it taste as if it came from a mountain spring.

We live in an age of convenience foods and household appliances. We do not have to slaughter pigs, pluck chickens, or make soap and candles. We do not hand-wash clothes. Machines often wash our dishes for us—and still everyone complains that they hardly have any time. The American family, we are told, is falling apart. It does not dine: it grazes from snack to snack.

I have no idea whether or not the American family is falling apart. I do know that many people still like to cook for their family, but that when they rush home after a day at the office they may not have a lot of time and energy to spend on cooking.

I am no superwoman, but I like to cook and I am lucky that I work at home. On the other hand, while I like a nice meal, I do not want to be made a nervous wreck in the process of producing one. I like dishes that are easy, savory, and frequently cook themselves (or cook quickly). I like to feel a little more ambitious on a weekend, when I have time to cook without too much interruption.

I do not believe that you have to spend a lot of money to eat well: it is hard to beat a plain old baked potato. But there are things it is worth spending money on. These are the accessories of cooking, the culinary equivalent of the beautiful handbag or wonderful shoes that make everything else look better. Sweet butter and really good olive oil are worth the money. So are high-quality vinegar (my own favorite is sherry wine vinegar from Spain), sea salt, fresh pepper and fresh herbs. For everyday use I like raw sugar, which tastes like sugar to me and not like some supersweet chemical. At holiday time I like to spring for a few fancy things—a little smoked salmon, some fancy biscuits or chocolate pastilles.

These essays were written at a time when it was becoming increasingly clear that many of our fellow citizens are going hungry in the streets of our richest cities. It is impossible to write about food and not think about that.

I hope that those who are lucky to be well fed will find this book useful in feeding family and friends.

Laurie Colwin
New York City, 1987

STARTING OUT
IN THE KITCHEN

C ooking is like anything else: some people have an inborn talent for it. Some become expert by practicing and some learn from books.

The best way to feel at ease in the kitchen is to learn at someone's knee. Years ago a child (usually a girl) would learn from her parent (usually her mother) by standing on a chair next to the stove and watching intently, or by wandering into the kitchen and begging to help. I was once given an amazing lunch by a young woman whose mother had been unable to boil water but was quite able to employ expensive Chinese help. Everyone should have the good fortune either to be Chinese or to be rich. Either way, you can end up learning how to make homemade won tons and duck stuffed with cherries and fresh lichee nuts.

For those who come to cooking late in life—by this I mean after the age of eighteen—many are the pitfalls in store. For instance, if you ask an experienced cook what dish is foolproof, scrambled eggs is often the answer. But the way toward perfect scrambled eggs is full of lumps. It is no easy thing to make perfect scrambled eggs, although almost anyone can turn out fairly decent ones, and with a little work, really disgusting ones can be provided.

I was once romantically aligned with a young man who I now realize was crazy, but at the time he seemed . . . romantic. It was on the subject of scrambled eggs that I began to have my first suspicions. He claimed his scrambled eggs resembled one of those asbestos mats you put over the burner to diffuse the flame. I asked him what his method of making them was.

"Well," he said, "I mash them together—you know what I mean—and then I add whatever spice is around."

I asked him what was usually around. Mace, he said, and ground thyme. He produced two very old-looking tins. I did not understand why a person would want to have mace in his eggs or ground thyme, which tastes like a kind of bitter, powdered sawdust and is not good for anything unless you need weird green powder for a prop. Well, then what? I wanted to know.

"I heat up a little vegetable oil in a pan and go and take a shower. When I come back, I put in the eggs and then I go and shave. By the time I'm finished shaving, they're done."

This should have been enough to make me flee, but love, aside from being blind, is also often deaf.

The loveliest scrambled eggs I have ever had were given to me by a not crazy young man, an Englishman who insisted that scrambled eggs should be made in a double boiler. The result is a cross between a scrambled egg and a savory custard, and if you happen to have about forty minutes of free time some day it is certainly worth the effort.

You scramble the eggs and add a tablespoon of cream. You then put a lump of butter into the top of a double boiler and when it melts, add the eggs. Stir constantly, remembering to have your blood cholesterol checked at the soonest possible moment. Stir as in boiled custard until you feel either that your arm is going to fall off or that you are going to start to scream uncontrollably. It is wise to have someone you adore talking to in the kitchen while you make these eggs, or to be listening to something very compelling on the radio. If you have truly mastered the art of keeping a telephone under your chin without its falling to the floor, a telephone visit always makes the time go faster.

The resulting eggs are satiny and creamy and do not need anything at all, although if your palate is jaded, these eggs can be made with cheese. I would recommend this dish, known to me as English Scrambled Eggs (although no one else I have ever met in England has ever heard of them), only to supervised beginners.

Or take beef stew, that favorite of Brownie and Girl Scout leaders for cooking projects. People are always messing it up, mostly men. A good cook I know was given something really awful by a fellow. It was stew all right, but the meat had the texture of jerky. She was curious and, after almost breaking a tooth, asked how he had achieved this strange leatherlike substance.

"The recipe said to sauté until brown," said the fellow. "So I did."

"And how long did you do it for?" she asked.

"Oh, an hour or so," he replied.

My own husband confessed to me that he was flummoxed by the instruction "Add liquid to cover." The result was a kind of gray water—rather like the gray-green, greasy Limpopo River in "The Elephant's Child" by Rudyard Kipling.

So much for the idea that if you can read you can cook.

Let's say you have never cooked a thing in your life but have made the mad, foolhardy gesture of inviting someone to dinner. Many years ago I worked with a girl whose fiancé did not know that she was unable to cook. They had a very proper courtship— separate apartments, theater dates and so on. Once a week he came for dinner and she could be heard on the telephone confabulating with a place called Casserole Kitchen, or Casserole Cottage, which sent over a homely-looking something or other and you sent back the empty pot. Years later I read her marriage announcement in the *Times* and wondered if Casserole Bungalow was still around or if she had learned to cook. More interesting, had she ever confessed to her husband?

Of course now that there is a fancy takeout shop on every corner, not knowing how to cook is no longer so problematic. My cousin's wife, a hardworking and elegant person, claimed for years that she did not apply heat to food, but she knew how to shop and, what is more, she knew where. Brunch at my cousin's is the only meal I have ever had at which everyone gets as much smoked salmon as they want.

My cousin's wife is an interesting case in point. She is an Italophile and decided that since she ought to learn to cook, Italian food was what she wanted to learn. She started rather simply with a combination of cooking and shopping. That is, she would apply heat to one dish and buy the rest. Little by little she has expanded her repertoire and it is now possible to get an amazingly good four-course dinner at her house.

One of her first attempts was lasagna, something notoriously difficult to concoct. Hers was a success, but she was in a state of nerves, which gives backbone to my theory that novices go for the elaborate.

The novice cook goes to the kitchen armed with a *chinoise* and a copy of *Edwardian Glamour Cooking Without Tears* in order to produce a lobster bisque made of pounded lobster shells, or invites a loved one for a dinner that begins with seviche and ends with a fruit soufflé.

The fact is, those nice simple things—a grilled steak or lamb chops, boiled potatoes, and steamed string beans—are quite formidable enough. The steak is either raw or grilled into shoe leather. The potatoes turn out crunchy in the center, never a good thing in a boiled potato, or mushy. The string beans are either underdone or they are overdone and have turned a limp olive green.

So what is the novice, quivering with anxiety and expecting some nice person to turn up hungry in a number of hours, to do? The novice should try some fairly easy dish that requires long cooking. The novice should consult several recipes and read them over a few times until he or she has gotten the parts straight in his or her mind. And the novice should call up the best cook he or she knows and listen to what that person says. *And then the novice should stick to it.*

I had a friend whose experience in the kitchen centered around opening cans of Irish potatoes and putting a hamburger into a pan while the frozen French-cut string beans were boiling. She got engaged to a very sociable fellow who liked to entertain, and she needed a party dish. I gave her my tried and true recipe for chili (which I got from the best cook I know) and explained every detail carefully. This is why a friend beats a cookbook hands down: you can't cross-examine a cookbook.

The day after the dinner party she called to say that the chili was kind of weird.

"Weird?" I said. "How could it be weird?"

"Well," she said, "as I was putting it together this guy called. He lives in Nebraska and I used to go out with him. He told me that he always put some cinnamon and turmeric in his chili, so I did."

My lessons in cooking came from my mother, a wonderful cook who makes, among other things, a savory, never-fail straightforward beef stew. As you gather courage, after cooking it a dozen times, you can begin to experiment and refine your technique. In no time at all you will be making true daube cooked between two sheets of pork rind with a calf's foot thrown in, but that is for later. This is for now.

EXTREMELY EASY
OLD-FASHIONED BEEF STEW

serves 2–3 with leftovers

1 cup white flour
2½ pounds stewing beef, cut in cubes
2 tablespoons paprika
black pepper
¼ cup olive oil
3 cloves garlic, chopped
2 carrots, scraped and cut in chunks
2 onions, quartered
2 cloves garlic, minced
2 medium Idaho potatoes, peeled or unpeeled,
cut in chunks
1 cup red wine
1 4-ounce can tomato sauce
2 tablespoons tomato paste

1. For two people I suggest two and a half pounds of stewing beef, which will provide leftovers. Have the butcher cut the beef into cubes. After a while you will do this yourself to get the exact size you want.

2. Put flour into a paper bag with paprika and three or four twists of the pepper grinder. Shake gently. Beef stew does not require salt.

3. Put half the cubes in the bag, shake, remove with your hands or a slotted spoon, and then add the rest and shake.

4. Heat olive oil in a skillet, turn down the flame, and fry the meat gently until the flour begins to turn color. It does not have to be evenly done. The true purpose of this is to add color and depth to the sauce.

5. Put half the meat into a deep casserole and sprinkle with half of the chopped garlic. Add one carrot, one onion quartered (one quarter stuck with two cloves of minced garlic), and one medium Idaho potato. Add the rest of the browned meat, another carrot, onion, potato and remaining chopped garlic.

6. Into the skillet pour wine, stir in tomato sauce and tomato paste. Cook down, stirring all the time (about four minutes), take off the fire and pour over the meat.

7. Cover the casserole and cook at 300° for at least three hours. You can put this in the oven and go about your business. Cook for the last fifteen minutes with the cover off.

You serve this with noodles, for which you follow the directions on the package. You can serve these noodles with butter, or with olive oil, or with grated cheese and chopped scallion.

As to the rest of the meal, it is simply too draining for a first-timer to provide everything. A salad requires only a bunch of watercress, some oil and vinegar, salt and pepper. If you have your heart set on baking a cake, invite friends in for dessert only and forget dinner. Step by step is the motto here.

And as every cook knows, and every cook was once a novice of some sort or another, you can always experiment on yourself and your loved ones.

Keep in mind that you should always apologize and never explain and that if the ultimate in horror takes place, there is one sure remedy.

Once upon a time some old friends of my husband's came for dinner. I had never met these people, and I had also never cooked those dry, filled tortellini you find in packages in Italian food shops. I have come to realize that these are meant for soup—or they ought to be—but I cooked a large pot of them and we all sat down.

It is a strange feeling to have pasta first crunch and then stick to your teeth, no matter how nice the sauce is. My husband and I exchanged glances. His friends, it was clear, had smoked a considerable amount of marijuana before coming to us, but even they noticed that something was funny.

"Hey," said one of these friends, "wouldn't it be groovy if we could dump this whatever-it-is in the garbage and go out for dinner?"

So that is what we did. If all else fails, eat out, and while you are smiling through your tears, remember that novices usually make the same terrible mistake only once.

THE LOW-TECH PERSON'S
BATTERIE DE CUISINE

How depressing it is to open a cookbook whose first chapter is devoted to equipment. You look around your kitchen. No *chinoise*! No flan ring! No salamander! How are you ever going to get anything cooked? What sort of a person is it who doesn't own a food mill?

I have been daunted for years by my lack of equipment. One summer in a rented country house I had a flirtation with my landlady's food processor and vowed to marry one when I got home. Why, it puréed the soup! It shredded the carrots in two seconds! How had I ever lived without one? Winter came and found me in my own kitchen pushing the cooked vegetables through an old strainer and grating the carrots with one of those cylindrical tin graters with patches for shredding, grating and slicing. As ever, next to the contraption is the box of Band-Aids, since it is impossible not to grate your knuckles as well.

Instead of a food processor, I have a couple of knives, the grater, and a blender that has four speeds (all the same, as far as I can tell). Until I went to a tag sale and found a food mill for three dollars, the kitchen strainer and the wooden pestle were all I had to help me purée the soup or the vegetables.

Until, at another tag sale, I bought a hand-held electric beater for fifty cents (thirteen years ago—bought secondhand and still going strong), what egg whites or cream was whipped by me got done with a whisk in an extremely heavy and uncomfortable copper pot. The copper pot is now a decoration, but I have retained the whisk. Every home should have one. For making lump-free polenta, cream of wheat or grits, there is nothing like it.

I do not have a toaster or a juicer. Three toasters have died on me and now I toast under the broiler. I do not have a cutlet bat, a pastry pin or a pastry bag. I wish I had a mandoline, but I do not. Instead I have my knives and the knuckle-scraping grater, which makes fine scalloped potatoes. I do not have a frying basket, a charlotte mold, a stockpot, a fish poacher or a terrine. I will never have a microwave oven because I believe they are dangerous, and totally unnecessary unless you are running a fast-food operation or, like one of my cousins, you are amused by watching eggs explode.

On the other hand, I have a number of mixing bowls, and since I have so little in the way of equipment, I have lots of room for them. I have come to believe that with a few wooden spoons and rubber spatulas (I have three) many things are possible.

Most things are frills—few are essential. It is perfectly possible to cook well with very little. Most of the world cooks over fire without any gadgets at all.

Here then, for people just starting out, is a list of what I consider essentials. It is wise to keep in mind that pots and pans are like sweaters: you may have lots of them, but you find yourself using two or three over and over again.

■ Two knives—one small, one large. The small cuts the vegetables, slices and pares. The large can be used to slice bread or carve the turkey or chop, as in a cleaver. These knives should be of carbon steel. Stainless steel is hopeless: it never takes a proper edge. There is no point whatsoever in a serrated knife which, in my experience, does *not* cut bread well. In fact, there is no point at all in anything that does only one job.

■ Two wooden spoons—a long-handled one and a short-handled one.

■ Two rubber spatulas. One wide, one narrow. These last only a couple of years and then the rubber heads fall off.

■ A decent pair of kitchen shears, which can also be used for sewing, cutting the flowers and opening parcels.

■ Two frying pans, one small, one large. The small is for cooking two eggs, a child's lunch, a toasted cheese sandwich. The big one is for big jobs—pancakes, chicken breasts and so on. An omelet pan is a wonderful thing to have, but a large frying pan can always be used instead.

■ Two cutting boards, one large, one small. The large is self-explanatory. The small is for mincing a clove of garlic, chopping a few sprigs of parsley or slicing one egg.

■ Two roasting pans. A big one for the turkey and a medium-sized one, preferably earthenware, which holds and distributes heat better for baking eggplant parmigiana, or roasting a chicken. Such a pan can double as a gratin.

■ Two soup kettles, one four-quart, one ten. Mine are white enamel over steel and come from the local hardware store. They have many uses: making soup, steaming vegetables, cooking spaghetti.

■ A heavy-lidded casserole, enamel over cast iron or earthenware, for stews and daubes and chili.

■ A pair of cheap tongs—no kitchen is complete without them. For picking up asparagus or other vegetables, for pulling the stuck spaghetti from the bottom of the pot, for grabbing cookies that have fallen off the sheet in the oven. Tongs can easily be unbent to form one long arm with which to retrieve things that you have accidentally kicked under the stove, and then they can be bent back into tongs again.

■ One all-purpose grater.

■ One little bitty grater, the size of a fly swatter, for grating a little cheese for the pasta, garlic, ginger or egg.

■ Mixing bowls. As far as I am concerned, the more the better, but three in a nest—small, medium and large—will do.

■ A sharp-pronged fork. This has endless uses and if it is good-looking enough it can be used to serve fried chicken.

Of course there are special interests that must be catered to. I own something called a chicken fryer—a large, straight-sided skillet with a domed top. I use it twice a year to fry chicken, and while it takes up space, it is the right tool for the job. I am also thinking of investing in a lemon zester, since my family is crazy about madeleines and the grater doesn't get enough zest off. My sister cannot live without her wok, a wonderfully versatile implement that I have never cozied up to.

As to baking, which requires a great deal of specific equipment, my motto is: never buy anything except at a tag sale. The tag, house or garage sale is the low-tech cook's happy hunting ground. People are constantly getting rid of bundt pans and springforms and bread tins. While it is true that you can always bake a meat loaf in a bread pan, a bundt pan is useful generally for making a bundt cake. My brioche mold cost two dollars and I have never paid more than fifty cents for a cake tin. A person might easily get along with a baking sheet, a muffin pan and a cake tin, but things get quickly out of hand when you start baking and one day you realize that you have acquired a tart ring, a couple of pudding basins and a madeleine pan and are hankering for a pizza tile.

But the world is full of people being ingenious. Most people have never heard of a *savarin* or a turk's head mold. I myself once cooked spaghetti in a champagne bucket, and while it is always nice to have a useful thing that does the job handily, it is a fact that you can do anything a food processor can do and do it even during a power failure.

Certain things are totally useless (a matter entirely of personal taste): the electric knife, the garlic press, the electric pasta machine, the pastry blender.

For those who own nothing but one knife and one pot, here is the ultimate one-pot meal, taught to me by a working mother.

SAUTÉED VEGETABLES AND POACHED EGG IN ONE POT

for 1 person

1 small green zucchini sliced
1 small yellow zucchini sliced
8 snow peas cut in thirds
1 small onion, sliced
butter
minced garlic, to taste
black pepper
1 or 2 eggs

1. Take the vegetables (the above combination, or whatever you like) and gently sauté them in butter with garlic. The idea is not to fry them but to get them tender. They should be partially covered to let out a little of their own juice.

2. Take the cover off, grind on some black pepper, push the vegetables against the sides of the pot (or pan or skillet: anything will do) and melt a little more butter. Break in one or two eggs, depending on how hungry you are, and cover until the eggs are cooked. They will have partially poached in the butter and vegetable liquor.

3. If you are civilized, you can arrange the vegetables on a plate and put the egg on top. If you are not, you can eat it right out of the pot. If you want some grated cheese, you can scrape it with your knife.

While you are eating this satisfying dinner (perhaps with your sharp little kitchen fork), you can reflect that the common kitchen knife can reduce nuts to powder, mince meat as well as any grinder with less mess, as well as shred the cabbage for cole slaw.

Always keep these points in mind:

■ If someone happens to give you one of those slicers that slices hard cheese, it can always be used as a spatula.

■ A double boiler is a handy thing to have but you will use its two separate parts more often than you will use it as a double boiler. A makeshift double boiler can easily be rigged up out of two pots.

■ A coffee grinder will grind nuts and spices and can be easily cleaned with a damp cloth.

■ In a pinch, you can always use a wine bottle as a rolling pin.

ALONE IN THE KITCHEN WITH AN EGGPLANT

For eight years I lived in a one-room apartment a little larger than the *Columbia Encyclopedia*. It is lucky I never met Wilt Chamberlain because if I had invited him in for coffee he would have been unable to spread his arms in my room, which was roughly seven by twenty.

I had enough space for a twin-sized bed, a very small night table, and a desk. This desk, which I use to this day, was meant for a child of, say, eleven. At the foot of my bed was a low table that would have been a coffee table in a normal apartment. In mine it served as a lamp stand, and beneath it was a basket containing my sheets and towels. Next to a small fireplace, which had an excellent draw, was a wicker armchair and an ungainly wicker footstool which often served as a table of sorts.

Instead of a kitchen, this minute apartment featured a metal counter. Underneath was a refrigerator the size of a child's playhouse. On top was what I called the stove but which was only two electric burners—in short, a hot plate.

Many people found this place charming, at least for five

minutes or so. Many thought I must be insane to live in so small a space, but I loved my apartment and found it the coziest place on earth. It was on a small street in Greenwich Village and looked out over a mews of shabby little houses, in the center courtyard of which was a catalpa tree. The ceiling was fairly high—a good thing since a low one would have made my apartment feel like the inside of a box of animal crackers.

My cupboard shelves were so narrow that I had to stand my dinner plates on end. Naturally, there being no kitchen, there was no kitchen sink. I did the dishes in a plastic pan in the bathtub and set the dish drainer over the toilet.

Of course there was no space for anything like a dining room table, something quite unnecessary as there was no dining room. When I was alone I ate at my desk, or on a tray in bed. When company came I opened a folding card table with a cigarette burn in its leatherette top. This object was stored in a slot between my countertop and my extremely small closet. Primitive as my kitchen arrangements were, I had company for dinner fairly often.

I moved in one cool summer day when I was twenty-three. That night I made dinner for two college friends who were known as the Alices since they were both named Alice and were best friends. I remember our meal in detail. A young man had given me a fondue pot as a moving-in present. These implements, whose real function was to sit unused on a top shelf collecting furry coats of dust, were commonly given as wedding and housewarming presents in the sixties and are still available at garage sales of the eighties. They were made of stainless steel and sat on a three-legged base at the bottom of which was a ring to hold a can of Sterno. Along with the pot came four long-handled forks, two of which I have to this day. (They are extremely useful for spearing string beans and for piercing things that have fallen onto the floor of your oven.) The fellow who gave it to me was fond of a place called Le Chalet Suisse, where I had once enjoyed beef fondue. I felt it would be nice to replicate this dish for my friends.

I served three sauces, two of which I made: one was tomato based and the other was a kind of vinaigrette. The third was béarnaise in a jar from the local delicatessen. I bought sirloin from the butcher and cubed it myself. When my two friends came, I lit the can of Sterno and we waited for the oil to heat.

While we waited we ate up all the bread and butter. One of the Alices began to eat the béarnaise sauce with a spoon. The other Alice suggested we go out for dinner. Once in a while we would dip a steak cube into the oil to see what happened. At first we pulled out oil-covered steak. After a while, the steak turned faintly gray. Finally, I turned one of my burners on high and put the pot on the burner to get it started. Thereafter we watched with interest as our steak cubes sizzled madly and turned into little lumps of rubbery coal. Finally, I sautéed the remaining steak in a frying pan. We dumped the sauces on top and gobbled everything up. Then we went to the local bar for hamburgers and French fries.

It took me a while to get the hang of two burners. Meanwhile, my mother gave me a toaster oven, thinking this would ensure me a proper breakfast. My breakfast, however, was bacon and egg on a buttered roll from an underground cafeteria at the Madison Avenue side of the Fifth Avenue stop of the E train. My toaster oven was put to far more interesting use.

I began with toasted cheese, that staple of starving people who live in garrets. Toasted cheese is still one of my favorite foods and I brought home all sorts of cheese to toast. Then, after six months of the same dinner, I turned to lamb chops. A number of fat fires transpired, none serious enough to call the fire department. I then noticed after a while that my toaster oven was beginning to emit a funny burnt rubber smell when I plugged it in. This, I felt, was not a good sign and so I put it out on the street. With the departure of my toaster oven, I was thrown back, so to speak, on my two burners.

Two-burner cooking is somewhat limiting, although I was constantly reading or being read to about amazing stove-top feats: people who rigged up gizmos on the order of a potato baker and baked bread in it, or a thing that suspended live coals over a pot so the tops of things could be browned, but I was not brave enough to try these innovations.

Instead, I learned how to make soup. I ate countless pots of lentil, white bean and black bean soup. I tried neck bones and ham hocks and veal marrow bones and bacon rinds. I made thousands of omelets and pans of my mother's special tomatoes and eggs. I made stewed chicken and vegetable stew. I made bowls of pickled cabbage—green cabbage, dark sesame oil, salt, ginger and lemon juice. If people came over in the afternoon, I made cucumber sandwiches with anchovy butter.

I would invite a friend or friends for Saturday night. Three people could fit comfortably in my house, but not four, although one famous evening I actually had a tiny dance party in my flat, much to the inconvenience of my downstairs neighbor, a fierce old Belgian who spent the afternoon in the courtyard garden entertaining his lady friends. At night he generally pounded on his ceiling with a broom handle to get me to turn my music down. My upstairs neighbor, on the other hand, was a Muncie, Indiana, Socialist with a limp. I was often madly in love with him, and sometimes he with me, but in between he returned my affections by stomping around his apartment on his gimpy leg—the result of a motorcycle accident—and playing the saxophone out the window.

On Saturday mornings I would walk to the Flavor Cup or Porto Rico Importing coffee store to get my coffee. Often it was freshly roasted and the beans were still warm. Coffee was my nectar and my ambrosia: I was very careful about it. I decanted my beans into glass and kept them in the fridge, and I ground them in little batches in my grinder.

I wandered down Bleecker Street, where there were still a couple of pushcarts left, to buy vegetables and salad greens. I went to the butcher, then bought the newspaper and a couple of magazines. Finally I went home, made a cup of coffee and stretched out on my bed (which, when made and pillowed, doubled as a couch), and I spent the rest of the morning in total indolence before cooking all afternoon.

One Saturday I decided to impress a youth whose mother, a Frenchwoman, had taught him how to cook. A recipe for pot roast with dill presented itself to me and I was not old or wise enough to realize that dill is not something you really want with your pot roast. An older and wiser cook would also have known that a rump steak needs to be baked in the oven for a long time and does not fare well on top of the stove. The result was a tough, gray wedge with the texture of a dense sponge. To pay me back and show off, this person invited me to his gloomy apartment where we ate jellied veal and a strange pallid ring that quivered and glowed with a faintly purplish light. This, he told me, was a cold almond shape.

The greatest meal cooked on those two burners came after a night of monumental sickness. I had gone to a party and disgraced myself. The next morning I woke feeling worse than I had ever felt in my life. After two large glasses of seltzer and lime juice, two aspirins and a morning-long nap, I began to feel better. I spent the afternoon dozing and reading Elizabeth David's *Italian Food.* By early evening I was out of my mind with hunger but feeling too weak to do anything about it. Suddenly, the doorbell rang and there was my friend from work. She brought with her four veal scallops, a little bottle of French olive oil, a bunch of arugula, two pears and a Boursault cheese, and a loaf of bread from Zito's bakery on Bleecker Street. I would have wept tears of gratitude but I was too hungry.

We got out the card table and set it, and washed the arugula in the bathtub. Then we sautéed the veal with a little lemon, mixed the salad dressing and sat down to one of the most delicious meals I have ever had.

Then, having regained my faculties, I felt I ought to invite the couple at whose house I had behaved so badly. They were English. The husband had been my boss. Now they were going back to England and this was my chance to say good-bye.

At the time I had three party dishes: Chicken with sesame seeds and broccoli. Chicken in an orange-flavored cream sauce. Chicken with paprika and brussels sprouts. But the wife, who was not my greatest fan, could not abide chicken and suggested, through her husband, that she would like pasta. Spaghetti alla Carbonara was intimated and I picked right up on it.

Spaghetti is a snap to cook, but it is a lot snappier if you have a kitchen. I of course did not. It is very simple to drain the spaghetti into a colander in your kitchen sink, dump it into a hot dish and sauce it at once. Since I had no kitchen sink, I had to put the colander in my bathtub; my bathroom sink was too small to accommodate it. At this time my bathroom was quite a drafty place, since a few weeks before a part of the ceiling over the bath had fallen into the tub, and now as I took my showers, I could gaze at exposed beams. Therefore the spaghetti, by the time the sauce hit it, had become somewhat gluey. The combination of clammy pasta and cream sauce was not a success. The look on the wife's face said clearly: "You mean you dragged me all the way downtown to sit in an apartment the size of a place mat for *this*?"

When I was alone, I lived on eggplant, the stove-top cook's strongest ally. I fried it and stewed it, and ate it crisp and sludgy, hot and cold. It was cheap and filling and was delicious in all manner of strange combinations. If any was left over I ate it cold the next day on bread.

Dinner alone is one of life's pleasures. Certainly cooking for oneself reveals man at his weirdest. People lie when you ask them what they eat when they are alone. A salad, they tell you. But when you persist, they confess to peanut butter and bacon sandwiches deep fried and eaten with hot sauce, or spaghetti with butter and grape jam.

I looked forward to nights alone. I would stop to buy my eggplant and some red peppers. At home I would fling off my coat, switch on the burner under my teakettle, slice up the eggplant, and make myself a cup of coffee. I could do all this without moving a step. When the eggplant was getting crisp, I turned down the fire and added garlic, tamari sauce, lemon juice and some shredded red peppers. While this stewed, I drank my coffee and watched the local news. Then I uncovered the eggplant, cooked it down and ate it at my desk out of an old Meissen dish, with my feet up on my wicker footrest as I watched the national news.

I ate eggplant constantly: with garlic and honey, eggplant with spaghetti, eggplant with fried onions and Chinese plum sauce.

Since many of my friends did not want to share these strange dishes with me, I figured out a dish for company. Fried eggplant rounds made into a kind of sandwich of pot cheese, chopped scallions, fermented black beans and Muenster cheese. This, with a salad and a loaf of bread, made a meal. Dessert was *always* brought in. Afterwards I collected all the pots and pans and silverware and threw everything into my pan of soapy water in the bathtub and that was my dinner party.

Now I have a kitchen with a four-burner stove, and a real fridge. I have a pantry and a kitchen sink and a dining room table. But when my husband is at a business meeting and my little daughter is asleep, I often find myself alone in the kitchen with an eggplant, a clove of garlic and my old pot without the handle about to make a weird dish of eggplant to eat out of the Meissen soup plate at my desk.

HOW TO FRY CHICKEN

As everyone knows, there is only one way to fry chicken correctly. Unfortunately, most people think their method is best, but most people are wrong. Mine is the only right way, and on this subject I feel almost evangelical.

It is not that I am a bug on method—I am fastidious about results. Fried chicken must have a crisp, deep (but not too deep) crust. It must be completely cooked, yet juicy and tender. These requirements sound minimal, but achieving them requires technique. I have been frying chicken according to the correct method for about ten years, and I realize that this skill improves over time. The last batch fried was far, far better than the first. The lady who taught my sister and me, a black woman who cooked for us in Philadelphia, was of course the apotheosis: no one will ever be fit to touch the top of her chicken fryer.

I have had all kinds of nasty fried chicken served to me, usually with great flourish: crisp little baby shoes or hockey pucks turned out by electric frying machines with names such as Little Fry Guy. Beautifully golden morsels completely raw on the inside. Chicken that has been fried and put into the fridge, giving the crust the texture of a wet paper towel.

I have also had described to me Viennese fried chicken, which involves egg and bread crumbs and is put in the oven after frying and drizzled with butter. It sounds very nice, but it is *not* fried chicken.

To fry chicken that makes people want to stand up and sing "The Star-Spangled Banner," the following facts of life must be taken seriously.

■ Fried chicken should be served warm. It should never be eaten straight from the fryer—it needs time to cool down and set. Likewise, fried chicken must never see the inside of a refrigerator because this turns the crisp into something awful and cottony.

■ Contrary to popular belief, fried chicken should not be deep-fried.

■ Anyone who says you merely shake up the chicken in a bag with flour is fooling himself. (More on this later.)

■ Fried chicken must be made in a chicken fryer—a steep-sided frying pan with a domed top.

■ It must never be breaded or coated with anything except flour (which can be spiced with salt, pepper and paprika). No egg, no crumbs, no crushed Rice Krispies.

Now that the basics have been stated, the preparation is the next step. The chicken pieces should be roughly the same size—this means that the breast is cut into quarters. The breast is the hardest to cook just right as it tends to get dry. People who don't quarter the breast usually end up with either a large, underdone half, or they overcompensate and fry it until it resembles beef jerky.

The chicken should be put in a dish and covered with a little water or milk. This will help to keep the flour on. Let the chicken stand at room temperature. It is not a good thing to put cold raw chicken into hot oil.

Meanwhile, the flour should be put into a deep, wide bowl,

with salt, pepper and paprika added to taste. I myself adore paprika and feel it gives the chicken a smoky taste and a beautiful color.

To coat the chicken, lay a few pieces at a time in the bowl and pack the flour on as if you were a child making sand pies. Any excess flour should be packed between the layers. It is important to make sure that every inch of chicken has a nice thick cover. Now heat the oil and let the chicken sit.

And now to the frying. There are people who say, and probably correctly, that chicken should be fried in lard and Crisco, but I am not one of these people. Fried food is bad enough for you. I feel it should not be made worse. The lady who taught me swore by Wesson oil, and I swear by it, too, with the addition of about one-fourth part of light sesame oil. This give a wonderful taste and is worth the added expense. It also helps to realize that both oils are polyunsaturated in case one cannot fry without guilt.

The oil should come up to just under the halfway mark of your chicken fryer. Heat it slowly until a piece of bread on a skewer fries as soon as you dip it. If it does, you are ready to start.

Carefully slip into the oil as many pieces as will fit. The rule is to crowd a little. Turn down the heat at once and *cover*. The idea of covering frying chicken makes many people squeal, but it is the only correct method. It gets the chicken cooked through. Remember that the chicken must be just done—juicy and crisp. About six minutes or so per side—and you must turn it—once is probably about right, although dark meat takes a little longer. A sharp fork makes a good tester.

When the chicken just slips off the fork, it is done inside. Take the cover off, turn up the heat, and fry it to the color of Colonial pine stain—a dark honey color. Set it on a platter and put it in the oven. If your oven is gas, there is no need for any more warmth than that provided by the pilot light. If electric, turn it up a little in advance and then turn it off. You have now made perfect fried chicken.

And you have suffered. There are many disagreeable things about frying chicken. No matter how careful you are, flour gets all over everything and the oil splatters far beyond the stove. It is impossible to fry chicken without burning yourself at least once. For about twenty-four hours your house smells of fried chicken. This is nice only during dinner and then begins to pall. Waking up to the smell of cooking fat is not wonderful.

Furthermore, frying chicken is just about the most boring thing you can do. You can't read while you do it. Music is drowned out by constant sizzling. Finally, as you fry you are consumed with the realization that fried food is terrible for you, even if you serve it only four times a year.

But the rewards are many, and when you appear with your platter your family and friends greet you with cries of happiness. Soon your table is full of ecstatic eaters, including, if you are lucky, some delirious Europeans—the British are especially impressed by fried chicken. As the cook you get to take the pieces you like best. As for me, I snag the backs, those most neglected and delectable bits, and I do it without a trace of remorse. After all, I did the cooking.

Not only have you mastered a true American folk tradition, but you know that next time will be even better.

POTATO SALAD

There is no such thing as really bad potato salad. So long as the potatoes are not undercooked, it all tastes pretty good to me. Some potato salads are sublime, some are miraculous and some are merely ordinary, but I have yet to taste any that was *awful*.

One of my earliest childhood memories is of going to lunch on a summer Saturday to Conklin's drugstore on the main street of Lake Ronkonkoma with my parents and sister. In those days, drugstores had booths, fountains and grills. They made bacon, lettuce and tomato sandwiches, fried eggs, egg salad, and hot fudge sundaes. What I remember most was the potato salad.

It was the standard American kind: potatoes and onions in a creamy mayonnaise dressing spiked with vinegar and black pepper: no chopped eggs, no celery. I still make this variety myself, with scallions substituted for onions and dill as an addition.

When I was young, potato salad was considered summer food. My mother made *her* mother's version, which included chopped celery and catsup in the dressing. It was known as pink potato salad and was served at picnics and barbecues as an accompaniment to fried or grilled chicken. No one would ever have thought of serving it in a formal setting.

Once I was out on my own and could cook to please myself, I figured that since I loved potato salad so much, other people did, too. I began to serve it to my friends at dinner parties.

"Oh, potato salad," they would say. "I haven't had any home-made in years!"

I gave it to them with thin sliced, peppery flank steak, and with cold roast chicken in the summer and hot roast chicken in the winter. It was always a hit.

For a while I turned my back on the old-fashioned kind and began to branch out. The possibilities were endless, since for every cook there are at least three potato salad recipes. I stole shamelessly from my friends. I made potato salad with funghi porcini, and with curried mayonnaise, and with chopped egg and walnut. But time after time I returned to my old standby: potatoes, scallions and dill. I must confess that I have never used homemade mayonnaise for this. I use Hellman's, cut with lemon juice.

Among cooks there is always discussion about the right potato. When in doubt, the new red potato comes close to being all purpose, but it does not *absorb* dressing the way an Idaho or russet does. The new red potato allows itself to be delicately coated with dressing. The mealier varieties soak it up like a sponge and thereby take more dressing. The result is creamier, but both are very good. Totally useless, in my opinion, is something billed as a salad potato: a soapy, greenish-looking creature which when cooked is waxy and watery at the same time—an unfortunate combination.

If you can find them, the tiny potatoes of spring are delicious. They are the size of quail's eggs and are wonderful steamed, cooled and eaten with a French olive oil, salt, pepper and a drop of lemon juice.

I have a friend, a man in his seventies who fled Vienna on the eve of World War II and ended up in Bogotá, who once every two years comes to New York. When I first met him, I invited him for dinner.

"What would you like me to cook?" I asked him.

"I am a meat and potatoes man," he said. "I want hamburgers and that wonderful American potato salad."

I said I did not approve of cooking hamburgers at home—that they were strictly restaurant food—but that I would make meat loaf. I told him that I made an especially good potato salad.

He appeared one July evening, dressed in a woolly sport coat. We begged him to take it off and he did, revealing a pair of snappy-looking suspenders. Thus liberated, he sat down to dinner. I watched anxiously, wondering what this *feinschmecker* would make of my potato salad.

"What do you think?" I said. I thought it almost perfect: creamy, oniony with just a jolt of vinegar.

"This is not at all what I had in mind!" he said forcefully.

"What do you mean?" I said. "This is A-plus American potato salad."

"I did not say it wasn't delicious," he said. "It is just not the potato salad I was thinking of."

"And what potato salad *were* you thinking of?"

"What they serve in the delicatessen around the corner from my hotel," he said. I knew the place. It was a Greek coffee shop.

"But Dr. Hecht," I said, "that stuff is made in five-hundred-gallon drums and sent all over the city."

"Exactly!" he said. "It tastes the same wherever I go. That is its charm."

He ate three helpings of mine, which mollified me enough to get me to admit that I liked the coffee shop variety myself.

The following are recipes stolen from friends.

KAREN EDWARDS'S WARM POTATO SALAD WITH STRING BEANS

serves 4

6 Idaho potatoes
½ pound string beans
¾ cup olive oil
1 teaspoon Dijon mustard
lemon juice (from one or two lemons)
garlic to taste
salt and pepper to taste
½ bunch chopped scallions

1. Boil the potatoes and steam the string beans.

2. Keep the potatoes warm. Cut the beans into longish pieces. Cut the potatoes—some of the skin will come off and some will stay on.

3. Make a vinaigrette—lots of it: combine olive oil, Dijon mustard, lemon juice, lots of garlic, salt and pepper to taste. The secret of this salad is lots and lots of dressing.

4. Dress the warm potatoes and beans, and add chopped scallions at the last minute.

ROB WYNNE'S POTATO SALAD WITH CRÈME FRAÎCHE

1. Cook as many new potatoes as you need, about three per person if small. Slice and cool.

2. Skin as many cucumbers (even if you are using kirbys) as will equal the amount of potatoes. Cut into julienne and drain.

3. Dress with a mixture of half mayonnaise, half crème fraîche, black pepper, and a hint of garlic.

My own potato salad is a snap. Idaho or new red potatoes can be used. Boil the potatoes. Make a dressing of Hellman's mayonnaise thinned with lemon juice and seasoned with black pepper. This does not need salt—prepared mayonnaise is quite salty enough. Mix the cut-up potatoes with chopped scallion and finely minced dill. Pour the dressing over and let sit for an hour or so before serving.

It is always wise to make too much potato salad. Even if you are cooking for two, make enough for five. Potato salad improves with age—that is, if you are lucky enough to have any left over.

FEEDING THE FUSSY

I will never eat fish eyeballs, and I do not want to taste anything commonly kept as a house pet, but otherwise I am a cinch to feed. My only allergy is a slight one to caviar, making me a cheap date. Furthermore, I am never on a diet regime I cannot be talked out of.

I am also not squeamish. Some years ago I was dared into eating something listed on a menu as "Half a Grilled Lamb's Head" in which you could see the little critter's teeth, and scoop the little grilled brains out of the little grilled brainpan, and I found it delicious, even as I stared at its poor little face.

I do not keep kosher and, therefore, I am a kind of universal recipient—the O Positive for hostesses. I can be fed in combination with anyone.

This cannot be said of most people. Most people are idiosyncratic about food. The restrictions, fads, diets, notions, and phobias people have about food are truly endless, to say nothing of serious religious conviction.

Every host and hostess has the same nightmare. A dinner party has been planned for six, of whom two are kosher. A menu has been invented around that fact: cold fish in green sauce, vegetarian lasagna, a salad and pear tart. At the last minute, it develops that of the other four guests, one is on a strict wheat-free diet, another cannot eat dairy products and another is allergic to fish.

An easy solution to this problem is to change friends instantly and find some red-blooded chowhounds with few scruples and no interest in health. Another approach is to take a preventative line: send out a questionnaire, or subject potential guests to ruthless cross-examination. "We're having a dinner party," you begin. "We're having the so-and-so's and we'd love you to come. Do you have any food phobias you would like to discuss? Have you recently discovered that you have any food allergies? Has your new naturopath doctor put you on any kind of diet we should know about in planning this meal? Have you recently taken up a new religion or gone back to your old one that has caused a change in your diet?" If you are wondering why you bought a home computer, you might now put it to good use and index your friends.

Some people have been taught that it is impolite to turn anything down, and if you ask them, they say: "Oh, I eat everything." Then, as you are slicing the steak, they shyly tell you that they have not eaten red meat in ten years.

It is also wise to know if people are fatally allergic to something. I know a woman who has a serious allergy to nuts. She spent her honeymoon in the hospital since the baker did not pay attention and slipped a little ground almond into the wedding cake frosting. You do not, of course, want to be responsible for the death of your guests, but sometimes it seems that they will be the death of you.

Vegetarians, for example, are enough to drive anyone crazy. Like Protestants, they come in a number of denominations. Lactovegetarians will eat dairy, eggs and usually fish, but some lactovegetarians will *not* eat fish. Vegans will not eat dairy products or eggs or fish. And some people say they are vegetarians when they mean they do not eat red meat, leading you to realize that for some people chicken is a vegetable.

On the subject of keeping kosher, there are degrees of strictness. Although they agree on a number of points—ritually slaughtered meat, no milk and meat together, no fish without scales, no pork—some Jews are more lax than others. I have friends who will have a meal in my house if they provide the food and I provide the paper plates and plastic forks. Others will eat a vegetarian meal. A few others will eat meat as long as it is kosher, prepared according to the dietary laws and cooked in a nonporous dish.

Finally, there are people who cannot eat certain things for reasons of health: people on salt-free diets, heart patients who must have polyunsaturated oil and no saturated fats whatsoever, and people with ulcers and other gastrointestinal disorders.

For those who have problems sleeping, making up menus for this range of problematic eaters provides lively late-night entertainment. If you do not have insomnia, fussy eaters in your social orbit will give it to you.

I have spent many white nights grappling with this problem and have come up with some foolproof, all-purpose answers.

For example, fruit salad. Everyone can eat this. Simply find out who is allergic to strawberries and leave them (or the strawberries) out. Fruit salad can be made year-round. In the summer, there is such a profusion of fruit that you must limit your choices. In the winter, the pickings are slimmer, but a wonderful fruit salad can be made with oranges, apples, pears and bananas, livened with kiwi fruit and some drained canned lichee nuts. This salad does not need sugar or liquor (but you can add both).

No one I have ever met is allergic to lettuce (although somewhere someone doubtless is), but some people simply will not eat salad. No matter, Bibb lettuce never harmed anyone, and even a heart patient may have a little olive oil. Salt-free dressing is not at all horrible if, to your oil and vinegar (or lemon juice), you add a little ground celery seed, some minced garlic and some dry mustard. Some people, however, really cannot ingest garlic and for them you must either make a separate dressing or serve them naked greens with oil and vinegar on the side.

Now for dinner. Here are two choices—one for meat eaters, one for vegetarians. This chicken dish can be fed to invalids, people recovering from abdominal surgery, heart patients and picky children.

CHICKEN
WITH CHICKEN GLAZE

serves 4

3 whole chicken breasts
spring water
cucumbers (½ hothouse or 8 medium kirbys)
chopped scallion (optional)

1. Split chicken breasts and remove every scrap of skin and fat. Leave the bone in.

2. Place in spring water, barely to cover. Add nothing—no onion, no garlic, no pepper.

3. Poach very slowly until very tender. Never allow to boil.

4. Remove the chicken, set aside to cool, and when cool, cut into strips.

5. Set the broth in a saucepan over medium high heat to reduce.

6. Meanwhile, cut cucumbers into julienne. Kirby or hothouse cucumbers are preferred—but if only those big waxed monsters from the supermarket are available, peel and seed. One will do. Place the cucumber on a platter and place the chicken on top.

7. Reduce the broth to a syrup. You now have chicken glaze. Pour this on top of the chicken and let sit until lukewarm. A refrigerated glaze will jell.

8. Chopped scallion on top is nice, unless someone can't eat it.

Now, for vegetarians of any stripe, people who keep kosher and those on macrobiotic diets. Pasta will not do; for some it is too fattening. Others can't eat wheat. Vegetable fritters would be nice except some won't eat eggs or fried food. A minimal approach is best: steamed vegetables with green sauce.

There is no limit to the quantity and combination of vegetables to serve. It depends on the number you are feeding, the vagaries of the season and what is in the market. Any and all vegetables will do. I like asparagus, snow peas, string beans, zucchini, yellow squash and broccoli. Simply steam until tender.

The sauce is a trick: it looks like and has the texture of mayonnaise, but it is not. This recipe was given to me by a friend with a tender stomach who has been on every health regime known to man.

JEANNETTE KOSSUTH'S GREEN SAUCE

1 bunch watercress
4 scallions (green part only)
1 large clove garlic (optional)
1 tablespoon Dijon mustard
½ cup olive oil (or ¼ cup olive oil,
¼ cup polyunsaturated oil)
freshly ground black pepper
lemon juice (from ½ lemon)

1. Cut stems from watercress (serve the tops with the steamed vegetables) and place in a blender with the green parts of scallions and garlic.
2. Add Dijon mustard, olive oil, pepper and lemon juice. Blend.
3. Garlic, which makes the sauce more delicious, can be omitted if one of your guests can't eat it. If you do use it, add it in Step 1.

Host- and hostessing, as we know, is often a heroic endeavor, requiring daring, ingenuity, a desire to take chances and a concern for others. These traits are also called for in saints and Nobel Prize winners.

And always keep this motto in mind: some are born fussy, and some have fussiness thrust upon them.

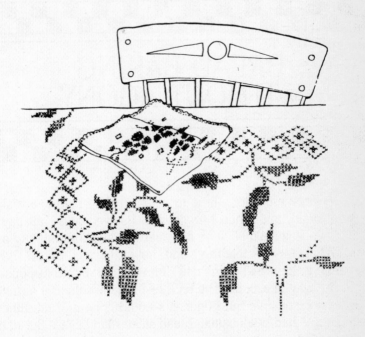

BREAD BAKING WITHOUT AGONY

I t took me a long time to get around to baking a loaf of bread, and when I finally did, I stayed home all day to do it. It seemed such a mysterious and intimidating process. What was "kneading" and how did you do it? What happened if the bread didn't rise? If it rose too much? Suppose it got in the way of a draft? The recipes I read assumed a familiarity I did not possess, but I figured it couldn't be *all* that difficult since people had been baking bread since man began. But to put me at my ease, I called in a more experienced friend to help me.

One gloomy winter day, we set about to bake. My friend insisted we do something called "setting the sponge"—that is, mixing up a little sugar and some of the flour with the yeast and water to get the yeast started. Then we sat around drinking coffee till the sponge got frothy. When the rest of the flour was added, my friend showed me how to knead by putting the dough on a floured surface, pushing it away from her, folding it over and pushing it away again, each time giving it a quarter turn. Very soon the dough had the springy, soft texture of a baby's bottom. I was very impressed.

We rolled the dough in soft butter and put it in a warm bowl, wrapped in a warm towel, in a warm place to rise, and while we waited we had elevenses.

About an hour or so later, we peeked under the towel and I learned what the term "doubled in bulk" means. The dough had grown to twice its size. The next thing to do was to "punch it down" (or "knock it down," as the English say). I found it very satisfying to give that puffy, balloonlike dough a good smack, which flattened it down at once. Then, as instructed, I kneaded it again. This time it was springier and seemed to come back at me. Again the dough was rolled in butter and put in a warm place, all dressed up in its protective snowsuit.

"Let's go out," I said.

"Oh, no," my friend said. "It isn't worth it. We'd have to turn around and come right back anyway."

By this time I began to feel fidgety.

"How much longer will this take?" I said.

"About another forty minutes to rise, and about an hour to bake," she said. "Let's have lunch."

We had lunch and then we played a desultory game of Scrabble, punctuated by punching the dough down again, forming it into loaves and slipping it into buttered loaf pans. We sat around a little while it rose a bit more, and then we baked it.

The result was a perfectly nice loaf of bread, but after spending an entire day in its service, I expected something a little more heroic.

After this marathon, I did not bake for some time, but I thought about it. I believed that everyone should know how to bake at least one kind of bread as a step toward self-sufficiency, and besides, the bread bought in the store was truly awful.

Then another friend gave me a recipe for a three-cup loaf that took one hour to bake, start to finish. I cut my teeth on this loaf, so to speak, and considering its density, it's a wonder I didn't knock them out. This loaf was *heavy* and tasted heavily of yeast.

Left out for a day, it developed into something that resembled a doorstop.

While I developed a craving for this bread, my affection was not shared, and after I had eaten a few slices, the rest of the loaf was left to languish and eventually produced a lush coat of furlike blue mold.

Nevertheless, I continued to bake it, and I gave it away to people, too. It is unknown what most of them did with it, but I did once bring a loaf as a house present and the expression on the face of my hostess made me finally realize how *unavailable* this bread looked.

Then I read a book that changed my life: *English Bread and Yeast Cookery* by Elizabeth David, with American notes by Karen Hess. I read it as if it were a novel: I took it to bed with me and stayed up late to finish it. I did read it as a house-bound person reads a travel book since I was now the mother of an eighteen-month-old daughter and I did not see how I could meet the demands of a loaf of bread and pay attention to a child at the same time.

But as I read I came across the interesting fact that bread dough will rise slowly and well at room temperature, which, considering the temperatures of most American houses, means a lukewarm place. If left to rise for a long time, only a small quantity of yeast is necessary. The process is rather like marination, and develops the taste of wheat (rather than the taste of yeast).

And then I read this liberating sentence:

It's really a question of arranging matters so that the dough suits *your* timetable rather than the other way around.

Why, you could have knocked me over with a pastry brush! This meant that I could mix up the bread in the morning, leave it to rise and actually go away! I could come home when I wanted, punch the dough down and let it rise all afternoon, if I needed to. Or I could take my daughter to the park, come home, punch the dough down, give it a short second rise and bake it during naptime. The idea that bread baking was something that would accommodate itself to me was downright thrilling.

The next morning I embarked on a Bloomer loaf—a whole-wheat baguette-shaped bread.

Unlike many recipes this one had no setting of the sponge and no proofing the yeast with sugar. The ingredients were flour, water, yeast, salt and a little milk.

Most recipes tell you to coat the dough with butter or oil (to keep it from sticking to the bowl). This recipe asked you to roll it in flour, which in my opinion gives a better crust. It is baked on a floured rather than a greased baking sheet.

And of course most recipes state that bread dough is fussy and must be treated with extreme care, put in a warm place and wrapped up tight. This recipe called for a warm bowl, a towel and a cool place.

I did as I was instructed, put the bowl on my dining room table, and then my daughter and I went about our business.

Three hours later we returned. I punched the dough down and gave it a second kneading, gave my daughter her lunch and put her in for her nap. An hour before she woke up, I formed the loaf, slashed the top with four diagonal cuts, brushed it with water and set it in the oven.

The result was absolutely breathtaking. I could not believe I had baked such a perfect loaf of bread: a dark brown crust, a beautiful smell. I let it cool down and when I cut it, it had air holes just like a loaf from a French bakery. Furthermore, it was delicious: wheaty, light but not at all airy. Everyone loved it, and I assumed it was beginner's luck.

It was not, for I have now made this bread over and over, with varying proportions of white to whole-wheat flour. I have added wheat germ or corn germ, made it with all water and no milk, let it rise all day, half a day, with a short first rise or a short second one. One afternoon I was about to leave the house when I realized that the second rising was probably over and I had forgotten about baking, so I punched the dough down again and let it rise a third time, and the resulting loaf was one dinner guests tore apart with their hands. The second best thing about this bread (the first is its taste) is that, unlike most things in life, it adjusts to you.

Before starting out there are a few things to consider. Although perfectly good bread can be made using whole-wheat flour from the supermarket, it goes without saying that the better the flour, the better the bread. Health food stores often stock excellent flours in bulk and there are mail order sources of first-rate flours, some of them organic. One such is Walnut Acres (Penns Creek, Pa. 17862), which has a bread flour that turns tan when water is added and makes an excellent loaf. There are often wonderful flours available at farmers' markets, and some people are lucky enough to live near a mill.

Sea salt is purer and saltier than any commercial salt, and it is not a mere nicety to use filtered water.

As for yeast, I use a preservative-free yeast from Walnut Acres which I buy in quantity and keep in the refrigerator. The finest loaves I ever made, however, used fresh yeast, which you can sometimes buy at the supermarket and sometimes beg from a friendly bakery.

Home-baked bread of any kind is better than anything you can buy at the grocery store. This, of course, is not saying much, since most commercial bread has the taste and texture of a cellulose sponge. Long-risen bread, however, is better than anything you can get even from a fancy bakery.

I have tinkered with the original recipe until I have found the bread I like best, one that manages to be dense and light at the same time:

FOR ONE LOAF

1½ cups unbleached white flour
1½ cups stone-ground whole-wheat flour
¾ cup coarse ground (or regular)
whole-wheat flour
1 heaping teaspoon salt
1 tablespoon wheat or corn germ
½ scant teaspoon yeast
¾ cup milk
¾ cup water

1. Into a large bread bowl put unbleached white flour, stone-ground whole-wheat flour and coarse ground whole-wheat flour (if you can't find coarse ground, simply add regular whole-wheat flour). Add salt and wheat or corn germ.

2. Mix yeast with 1½ cups liquid—¾ cup milk, ¾ cup water, or more water than milk—whatever you have to hand. (If you are going to leave it overnight, use ¼ rather than ½ teaspoon yeast.)

3. Pour the liquid into the flour and stir it up. The dough should be neither dry nor sticky but should tend more toward the sticky than the dry. If too sticky, knead in a little more flour.

4. Knead the dough well, roll it in flour, put it in a warm bowl (although I have put it in a regular old bowl right off the shelf). Leave it in a cool, draft-free place and go about your business.

5. Whenever you happen to get home, punch down the dough, knead it well, roll it in flour and forget about it until convenient.

6. Sometime later (with a long first rise, a short second rise is fine, but a long one is fine, too), punch the dough down, give it a final kneading, shape into a baguette, slash the top with four diagonal cuts, brush with water and let proof for a few minutes (and if you haven't the time, it can go straight into the oven).

7. You can preheat the oven or put it in a cold oven, it matters not a bit. Bake at 450° for half an hour. Turn the oven to 425° and bake for another twenty minutes.

Bread like this will astonish your friends. It makes a perfect house present. Even if the crust splits during baking, it is still a wonderful-looking loaf. The actual man work, so to speak, is under half an hour. The yeast does the rest for you.

You, of course, get all the credit.

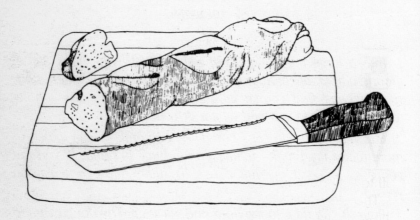

FRIDAY NIGHT SUPPER

We live in a decade that worships speed: fast food, one-minute managers, sixty-minute gourmets, three-minute miles. We lace up our running shoes and dash off to get on the fast track.

These days we are surrounded by overabundance but admire the minimal: *cuisine minceur*, high-tech design, thinness. We are far too busy to linger over a long, languid meal. Instead, we bolt a pint of yogurt and suit up for a five-mile run or a corporate takeover.

Food is now glamorous. Glossy magazines display tiny specks of underdone duck breast lying on oversized plates with the same reverence once lavished on models wearing Balenciaga dresses. This is the age of high-fashion food. Half a braised quail, a thimble of polenta and a sprig of cilantro are supposed to make you feel not satisfied but superior. A quick meal in a sleek white restaurant in which the portions are hummingbird-sized and the noise is deafening leaves plenty of time for a good forty-five minutes on the exercise bicycle whilst reading the *Wall Street Journal*.

But when all is said and done, man cannot live on charred monkfish and grilled baby vegetables alone. Every now and again even the fastest of the fast trackers must rest.

The old days were slower. People buttered their bread without guilt and sat down to dinner *en famille*. After a hard week of work, people welcomed the Sabbath and ushered it in with a big meal that took a long time to eat and longer to digest.

For those who have let it lapse, Friday night supper is a tradition worth reviving. It is a night when the heart of even the most assimilated Jew cries out for something more substantial than one skinless chicken breast. The traditional Friday night fare—pot roast and potato pancakes—is not something you would want to make a steady diet of, nor would you be comfortable serving it to your cardiologist. But it is truly heartwarming.

Many people, of course, have less than pleasant memories of Friday night dinners during which they were offered plates of weathered roof shingles accompanied by fried shoe heels. I myself had such a dinner at the home of a college friend in 1962 and I often wonder how her mother got her pot roast to that dire combination of overcooked and rubbery at the same time. I am still digesting that meal.

The trick is to make really good pot roast and potato pancakes. The pot roast must be tender enough to mash with a fork but should not, on the other hand, have the texture of shredded rope. The gravy must be thick and savory, without a speck of flour. As for the potato pancakes, they should have the texture of Florentine cookies—lacy and crisp. They ought, as a beau of mine once said, to go straight from the plate to your bloodstream. A side dish of applesauce is traditional and is a snap to make as it actually cooks itself.

And now, into the kitchen.

The crucial issue with pot roast is what cut to use. My mother favors front-cut brisket, but she grew up when one could buy prime meat and fancy cuts without dipping into capital. By the time I got around to serious cooking, a substantial meat purchase seemed as daunting as buying an ermine stole. Therefore

I settled on the cheaper chuck steak, cut thick, and I stand by it. It is fattier than brisket and therefore more lip-smacking. Five pounds will do for four people with a little left over. If you are feeding ravenous beasts or contemplate a weekend of cold pot roast sandwiches on rye, order more.

The following pot roast is a variation on the traditional but it is every bit as good.

FRIDAY NIGHT POT ROAST

serves 4–6

1 5-pound chuck steak
paprika
olive oil (preferably dark and fruity)
3 ripe red peppers
2 medium yellow onions
1 large carrot
1 fresh hot pepper (optional)
6 large cloves garlic
1 glass red wine
1 6 oz. can tomato sauce
black pepper

1. Take the chuck steak, tie a string around its middle and roll it on all sides in paprika.

2. Heat some olive oil in a skillet and sear the meat on both sides. Transfer it to a Dutch oven slightly larger than the meat.

3. Cut red peppers into strips and sauté them in the skillet. Add them to the meat along with the onions cut in quarters, the carrot sliced into chunks and, if you love hot food, a fresh hot pepper. Since there is never enough garlic, I use six big cloves but this can be adjusted to taste.

4. Into the skillet pour the wine and tomato sauce and cook down to thicken a bit. Pour over the meat, grind on some black pepper and cover. Cook in a slow oven (300°) until tender. That will take somewhere between three and five hours, so relax.

5. When the meat is done, remove the vegetables with a slotted spoon and push them through a sieve or run them through a food mill. A blender will not do. *The idea is to create a purée free of fibers, onion and pepper skins, and the twiggy bits of the hot pepper.*

6. Put the purée in a saucepan, add the meat juice and cook, over a moderate flame, until you have a thick gravy.

7. Slice the pot roast at the last minute and spoon the gravy over it, saving some for the gravy boat.

People often eat this in total silence in which case you may assume that you are not going to have any leftovers.

Now on to potato pancakes with a digression about vegetables.

Real potato pancakes must be fried in chicken fat, but if you clutch your breast at the thought of all that saturation, a combination of chicken fat and vegetable oil works perfectly. You can also kid yourself that while the chicken fat is coating your arteries, the polyunsaturates in the vegetable oil are cleaning them out. Some supermarkets have chicken fat in the dairy case, but it is usually filled with preservatives. It is cheaper to make it at home, as follows:

HOW TO RENDER CHICKEN FAT

1. Take the fat from one large chicken, dice it up and put it in a cold skillet.

2. Gently warm the skillet on a low fire. Meanwhile, dice one small yellow onion.

3. As soon as the fat begins to let down, turn the fire up slightly and add the onions.

4. Turning the flame up again (you want a medium flame), cook until the onions are brown (not burnt) and the fat has been completely rendered and the cracklings are crisp. What you now have, in addition to onion-flavored chicken fat, are called Grieben—*German for crackling. These must be terrible for you because they are so extremely delicious. Remove them with a slotted spoon from the fat, and if you can restrain yourself from eating them all as you stand there in the kitchen, use them to flavor the brussels sprouts:*

1. Trim the brussels sprouts (two one-pint boxes will feed four amply) and steam for ten minutes. Some people put a cross-hatch on the bottom but I consider this a frill, like skinning tomatoes. The idea here is to blanch, not cook.

2. Put the sprouts in an earthenware pan, cover with the Grieben *and shake until each sprout has had intimate contact with the cracklings. Add salt and pepper to taste and bake for two hours, shaking the pan from time to time. (You can put them on the rack under the pot roast.) You want sprouts that are golden brown on the outside and mushy on the inside. Even brussels sprout haters have been known to love these.*

It is silly to pretend that potato pancakes are dietetic or that they are good for you. If you are going to enjoy them, approach them as a rare delicacy, throw caution to the wind and have a good time. The following is my mother's recipe, a classic.

ESTELLE COLWIN SNELLENBERG'S
POTATO PANCAKES

serves 4-6

¼ cup chicken fat (see p. 52)
½ cup vegetable oil
5 medium Idaho potatoes
1 medium yellow onion
1 egg
1 tablespoon flour (or matzo meal)
¼ teaspoon baking powder
1 teaspoon cold water

1. *Put chicken fat and vegetable oil in a frying pan on a low flame.*

2. *Peel potatoes and hold in cold water.*

3. *Peel onion.*

4. *Quarter the onion and the potatoes. Feed the potatoes into the blender a few at a time, adding the onion, egg, flour (or matzo meal) and the baking powder dissolved in a teaspoon of cold water. Blend to a batter.*

5. *When the fat is hot enough to fry a piece of bread, start frying. Some like big pancakes and some like small. I like about a soupspoon of batter. Work fast, as potato batter has a dismaying tendency to start changing color—from pink to green to black.*

6. *Fry the pancakes until golden on both sides, drain on paper towels and keep on a hot platter in a hot oven. It is best to make them at the last minute, keeping them in the oven for the shortest time possible. They are, of course, best eaten directly from the skillet without any thought of sharing them with others.*

Applesauce is traditional, and while there are many brands available in the supermarket, homemade is so simple to make that it almost does not require a recipe, but for those who have never attempted it, here are the steps:

HOMEMADE APPLESAUCE

1. Peel and core any number of apples. Make as much as you like. A variety of apples—McIntosh, Granny Smith, Empire and so on—makes a very nice sauce. If you are using organic apples, don't bother to peel them and the result will be a lovely apple pink.

2. Put the apples in a heavy pot over a low flame and add half a cup of apple cider. Cover and cook slowly, stirring once in a while. The whole process takes under an hour.

3. If you like lumpy applesauce, mash the apples with a fork. If smooth, run them through a food mill or push them through a sieve. Either way, it is delicious.

After such a meal, a green salad is a must. I like to add a few bitter greens such as chicory or endive for balance, with a very simple oil and vinegar dressing.

As for dessert, there is only one dessert to have:

ORANGE AMBROSIA

Orange ambrosia is often called Bride's Dessert because it is so easy—nothing more than sliced oranges prettily arranged with a little garnish. It is of southern origin and now out of fashion, but I love it. After all that red meat and chicken fat, oranges are just the thing.

1. Peel six navel oranges. Get off as much of the white skin as you can and slice into very thin rounds. Arrange prettily on a glass plate (a glass plate is traditional).

2. Sprinkle with bourbon or Cointreau or tangerine brandy and let sit in the refrigerator. The idea is to get the oranges really cold.

3. Half an hour before serving, sprinkle with a little shredded coconut. The traditional garnish for this is a maraschino cherry, but (for those who fear red food dye) a slice of kiwi fruit, a Bing cherry or a flower looks just as nice. I have seen orange ambrosia decorated with violets, which is very attractive if you happen to have a supply of violets on hand.

This meal, which takes some time to prepare, must be eaten slowly. Afterwards it is best to stretch out on the sofa, balancing a cup of coffee on your stomach.

For the next month you may vow to eat nothing but brown rice and broiled fish, but on a cold Friday night, with the candles lit and a white cloth on the table, it is good to celebrate your good fortune in living comfortably and to remember those who do not.

In short, it is a time to count blessings, to savor life without rush and to end the work week happy, drowsy and content.

HOW TO DISGUISE VEGETABLES

I t is amazing how many adults hate vegetables. Mothers of small children are constantly complaining that their little darlings will not touch any green or yellow thing. By the time children reach twenty, however, you figure they might come around, but many don't. Some ignore their vegetables, some actively loathe them and some feel that a couple of baby string beans are the price they have to pay for soft-shell crabs.

I am lucky to have a child who adores almost everything. Both her parents adore their vegetables, too, but many children of vegetable-loving households live entirely on peanut butter and jelly sandwiches and even shun corn, that childhood favorite. It was from my child that I rediscovered how good plain steamed vegetables are, and I will never forget the look of delighted surprise on her face at her first taste of zucchini.

But many people are not delighted or surprised by zucchini or any other vegetables, and if you are going to serve them, you have to be crafty.

One very obvious trick is to make some delicious sauce—

hollandaise, mayonnaise or béarnaise—to dip the vegetables in. A person who dunks an asparagus spear into a puddle of homemade mayonnaise will end up eating the asparagus unless you have on your hands the kind of hard case who will *lick* the sauce off and then stick the asparagus back in for more.

A more effective way is to turn the offending vegetable into a fritter. Most people think fried food is *fun* and not serious eating. A crisp little fritter slips right down (often as a mere vehicle for the catsup or tomato sauce), but never mind that it is fried: it is all for a good cause.

Zucchini make wonderful fritter material, especially small, young ones roughly the size of a lead pencil. If necessary you can use those enormous overgrown zucchini that gardeners are always palming off on their friends in the fall.

Shred the zucchini—use four small ones—and drain it on a towel. Separate two eggs and beat the whites until fairly stiff. Add half a cup of milk to the egg yolk, beat and add about half to three-quarters of a cup of flour—the batter should be a little thicker than pancake batter. Add the zucchini, salt, pepper and some chopped scallion. Fold in the egg whites and fry in clarified butter (or unclarified butter) or olive oil until golden on both sides. Some people like large fritters. I like mine the size of a demitasse saucer. Of course these are not fritters in the strict sense of the term. Rather they are pancakes. As to their being fried, my motto about fried vegetables is: "Fried eggplant today, ratatouille tomorrow!"

Now to broccoli. How some people hate it! However, it turns into a sleek, rich pasta sauce. First you steam it. Then you sauté it in dark green olive oil with two cloves of garlic until the garlic is soft. Then you toss it all in the blender with pepper, a pinch of salt, the juice of half a lemon, more olive oil and serve it on penne or ziti or fusilli with lots of grated cheese, and no one will suspect what is being served.

People who are not paying close attention can be fooled by carrot pudding, a simple dish of puréed carrots, butter, one beaten egg and a pinch of nutmeg baked in a buttered pudding mold. Vegetables in this unnatural state—purées and timbales—often go unnoticed but eaten since the victim is not confronted by the dread thing itself.

Specific hatreds, however, should never be trifled with. People who will not (or say they will not) eat vegetables at all are fair game, but someone with a profound hatred, say, of beets should not be challenged. A life without beets or lima beans is a fine, full life. But to forgo leeks, collard, broccoli, string beans, escarole, and the vast profusion of beautiful green, yellow and purple vegetables stems from a prejudice that must be challenged.

Not enough has been written on the subject of our denatured produce, although John and Karen Hess's *Taste of America* addresses this topic quite depressingly. Read it and weep, and then go directly to your nearest farmers' market and try to find some Delicata squash to cheer you up. I have never seen it in any market except my local green market. This oblong squash is a muted orange with green streaks. As with most vegetables (except carrots), the smaller the sweeter is the rule. This sweet, lip-smacking squash makes even the tastiest butternut seem tasteless and weak. When vegetables have such flavor, you do not have to fool anyone. You simply ask them to taste and watch their faces. In an instant, the contents of the dish disappear and you are faced with demand but scant supply. Delicata squashes are excellent baked with butter and pepper or steamed and served with a drip or two of olive oil. If all our vegetables were so full of flavor, drastic measures would not have to be resorted to in order to get people to eat them.

There is, however, one drastic measure so rich that it makes a person groan. I myself am addicted to this recipe, which calls for shredded yams, egg, flour, hot red pepper flakes, chopped scallion and fermented black beans. This unlikely combination is sublime:

YAM CAKES WITH HOT PEPPER AND FERMENTED BLACK BEANS

These, like fried eggplant or zucchini, often do not reach the dining table.

serves 4

1 large yam
2 eggs
4 tablespoons flour
1 chopped scallion
red pepper flakes to taste
2 teaspoons fermented black beans
olive oil

1. *Shred the yam.*
2. *Beat up eggs, add to the potatoes and mix.*
3. *Add flour to make the mixture cohere (or more to make more coherent).*
4. *Add scallion, red pepper flakes and fermented black beans.*
5. *Form into cakes with a spoon (these fall to pieces rather easily. I use a bouillon spoon and press the mixture in) and fry in olive oil.*

Fermented black beans are available in Chinese grocery stores. They are pungent and salty and come mixed with salted ginger. They are wonderful with sautéed eggplant for a pasta sauce, and excellent sprinkled on top of a homemade pizza. Since they are very, very salty a few go a long way.

While you are concocting these things, remember that vegetables really are good for you and that every step, no matter how devious, should be undertaken to encourage people to eat them happily. You should not tell your hapless victims how you have duped them. This will only make them belligerent, which is not the idea at all.

You must not make speeches about health or hector people who insist on being pig-headed. Nor should you make lofty declarations, after the zucchini fritters have disappeared, about the good you are doing. As we know, the only thing that butters a parsnip is butter.

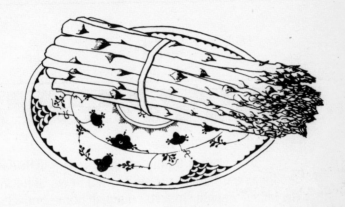

FISH

I do not come from a family of adventurous fish eaters. When I was a little girl, we ate broiled fillets of flounder, or my father brought smoked butterfish home from Barney Greengrass in New York, or, in the summer, we would go crabbing at Blue Point, on Long Island.

Crabbing is perfect child sport. You sit still for a very short time holding a string on the end of which is a piece of herring. In your other hand you hold a net. Very soon crabs begin to cruise the herring and you scoop them up. We came home from these excursions sunburnt and happy, with peach baskets packed with seaweed and blue crabs. Fixed in my memory of childhood is the wonderful time when the catch was so enormous we ran out of peach baskets and had to put the last crabs in a cardboard box. Halfway home, claws began to emerge through the cardboard. The boxes and baskets were brought into the kitchen while my mother put an enormous pot of water and crab spice on the stove. Just as it began to boil, the crabs in the cardboard ate their way through and escaped under the stove.

The best way to eat crabs, as everyone knows, is off newspaper at a large table with a large number of people. Adults drink beer. Children quaff iced tea. The crabs are boiled, drained and dumped in the center of the table (protected first by oilcloth and many layers of newspaper). Two people share a nutcracker and there are picks for everyone.

On birthdays we went to The Riverside Inn in Smithtown and ate lobster and Baked Alaska. On cold nights my mother baked salmon loaf, that wholesome staple of the late forties. In season we had what we called chicken of the sea, which others call sea squab, but are really blowfish.

The blowfish is a little critter with a poisonous liver and ovaries. What you eat is the back—a firm, plump morsel of meat with one central bone that looks like a minuscule edition of one of those old-fashioned combs with teeth on both sides. When I was little, we ate blowfish breaded with crumbs and fried. Last year at my local farmers' market, blowfish made an appearance in my life for the first time in years: there on ice was the food of my childhood. I bought some thinking they would be a nice treat for a small child.

These blowfish were an enormous hit with my little daughter, so I decided to sauté the rest in butter and garlic and serve them to adults. They were sweet, nutlike and delicate, and I served them continually through the spring, summer and early fall and was met with cries for more. We were very sad when the season ended, and very happy when it began again.

The only other fish I remember eating as a child was sea bass, cooked for me by a friend of my parents. I did not have sea bass again for close to thirty years—this is the result of not being drawn into fish stores—but it was as I remembered it. Now that striped bass are taboo, sea bass abound to keep us all happy.

As an adult I edged my way toward fish because my best friend's husband liked to get up at four in the morning, drive to Montauk and surf cast. One day he decided it would be a swell idea if we all piled into the car, took a series of motel rooms and went jigging for bass.

On the way we stopped for dinner at a roadside diner where I was given an entire small flounder. I had never eaten anything but a fillet before and this flounder seemed to me quite another thing altogether.

The next day we went trawling around in the tidal rip, armed with long poles with which we drove ourselves crazy jigging for bass—pushing those poles back and forth in a sideways motion hoping that something would bite one of our lures. Several of our party, after a few hours of gas fumes and circling, turned a faint olive color and decided to lie down. I drank a cup of awful coffee and then began to jig again. I was placidly jigging, thinking my own thoughts, when I suddenly felt that my arm was being pulled out of its socket. I yelped loudly to this effect. My friend's husband ran to my side.

"Hold on tight!" he said. "You've got one."

"You hold on tight," I said. "You're three times my size."

He gave me a look and I could see I had let him down in the real-man department.

I hung on for a while and he hung on too.

"Why is this fish trying to pull my arm off?" I said.

"They're fighting fish," he said. "That's the fun."

I did not find this lots of fun, and I found it less fun when the poor fish was hauled up on deck and flopped around desperately.

By the end of the day we had caught three eight-pound stripers and one of them was mine. My friend and her husband had a room with a kitchen, so we all repaired to our own rooms to shower and agreed to meet in their room to cook.

As I stepped out of my room, clean and dressed, I saw my friend's husband—an enormous, handsome fellow—sitting on a grassy bank, gutting the fish with a Japanese knife. He was as happy and absorbed as a child, and he smiled like a child as he flung the fish guts up to the circling gulls. He seemed a man entirely at peace, leaving me to wonder why I had given up vegetarianism at the age of seventeen.

But there, on the counter of the kitchen, was that beautiful big striper, cleaned, scaled and ready to bake. It was stuffed with scallion greens, garlic and some shreds of lean bacon, doused with a little white wine, dotted with butter and then swaddled in tin foil and baked in the oven. While it baked, we ate several buckets of steamers. In a small pan, we made a reduction of chopped bacon, butter, white wine and garlic, strained it and dribbled it over the fish when it was cooked.

Seven people polished off an enormous amount of that eight-pound fish. The next morning, I finished the cold remains and realized how delicious cold striped bass was. But those days are over and gone until our waters are clean and the striped bass population is no longer in danger.

I now find myself a fish lover, but I am still not a very adventurous fish cooker. Fish in my opinion should be grilled, broiled, sautéed in butter or turned into fish cakes. For large numbers of people I like to bake salmon fillets, and for less ceremonial occasions I like baked codfish served with green almond sauce. This is easily made by putting scallion greens, chopped blanched almonds, garlic, lemon juice, watercress bottoms and a hot green pepper into the blender with enough olive oil to make a sauce—it is delicious on a bland fish like cod or scrod.

I have cooked tilefish, red snapper, halibut, gray and lemon sole but I have never learned to like trout and I find bluefish quite inedible. I will confess I fear smaller fish that have to be cooked in one piece, like porgy, because I fear bones and because I can never get the skin crispy. But fresh sardines are worth the effort and the bones. Fried in butter they are incomparable. Mostly I stick happily to that which can be either filleted or cut into steaks.

Eating habits change, often for the better, with the acquisition of a child. We became a fish-eating family when our daughter began to eat solid food and developed a craving for such expensive things as salmon and sole. It is amazing how much salmon a child three or under can pack away.

As an entertainment after a morning at play group, the local mothers would wheel their babies into the fish store and amuse them by picking up the smaller fish and displaying them. Then we bought our fillets and went off to cook our lunches. The fish men were extremely cheerful and forbearing about this.

One morning one of my friends took her two-and-a-half-year-old daughter to the fish store. The fish man, an unshaven, unsmiling person, turned to the child.

"Whaddya want," he barked.

"Slamber," she said without batting an eye.

"What color is it?"

"Pink and green," said the child.

"Oh, yeah?" he said. "Well, we don't carry it."

"Then give me something else," said the little girl.

We eat quite a lot of slamber these days, which turned out to be salmon, and I remember my daughter's first taste of it. She smiled a smile of almost giddy delight, which made me realize how as we acquire experience things stop being so amazing.

About a million years ago I was taken out to dinner by a professor of Chinese studies. He took me to a real Chinese restaurant (as opposed to one of those places full of plastic dragons and chow mein) in Chinatown and proceeded to order one of the most fabulous dinners I had ever eaten. This food was news to me, rather like my daughter's first taste of salmon.

First we had hot and sour soup. My companion informed me that in China ox blood is dripped on the top of the hot soup in lines to make a design. Then we had a small order of fried dumplings and a small scallion pancake. I had not known that such things existed. Our next dish was sautéed lamb with scallions, but the centerpiece of the meal was a striped bass, steamed with black mushrooms, strips of ginger, scallion and Smithfield ham. At the first taste of that fish, I began to laugh. My companion gave me a worried look. After all, I was in my early twenties and perhaps he thought I was more than a little cracked.

But it was the food that made me laugh. It was so wonderful and unexpected, so totally new I hardly knew how else to respond.

Part of the experience of being a parent is the reexperiencing

of your own childhood, and as I watch my daughter taste her
first this and that—which, in New York City, means her first
shiitake mushroom, falafel, plate of hummus, tree ear, bamboo
shoot or chocolate mousse—I remember back to that time when
my palate was clear and unsophisticated, everything was an
adventure and the world was as fresh as a fish.

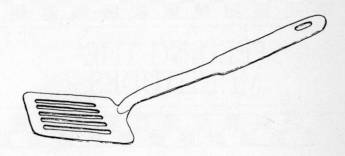

FEEDING THE
MULTITUDES

S omehow or other I always end up in a kitchen feeding a
crowd. At parties, I gravitate toward a platter or stack
of dishes or can be found hanging around the kitchen
being helpful. For the socially timid, the kitchen is the place to
be. At least, it is a place to start.

The idea of feeding a crowd is far from alien to me. Each year
my assimilated parents gave a Christmas Eve buffet, with turkey,
ham, three hot dishes, salad, petits fours, fruitcake, champagne
punch with peaches, eggnog and chocolate-covered orange peel,
with black caviar for an hors d'oeuvre.

At college, in an extremely crummy kitchen (a drainboard-
sized space in an off-campus men's dorm where two enterprising
fellows had formed a sandwich concern), my friend Michelle Reis
and I were paid cigarette money to make dozens of tuna fish
and cheese sandwiches to feed young ladies after curfew—this
was many hundreds of years ago when girls still had curfews at
college, although the curfew at our progressive school was considered to be extremely liberal. After twelve thirty these boys showed
up at the girls' dorms and sold our sandwiches at a hefty markup.

Reis and I—we were called by our last names exclusively—mixed enormous cans of tuna fish with large scoops of mayonnaise from an industrial-sized jar. We laid out the bread like a deck of cards, and spread the slices with iceberg lettuce leaves. The way to get the core out of a head of iceberg lettuce, we were instructed, was to bonk it forcefully on a counter. The core would then pull right out, and that, in my opinion, is all anyone needs to know about iceberg lettuce, except that when a head of it falls to the floor, it bounces, ever so slightly.

I was an early college dropout. When I dropped back in, it was to the School of General Studies at Columbia, where, in 1968, Students for a Democratic Society called a strike and occupied a number of buildings. I was a part-time student, part-time office girl, and when the strike was called I found myself in my Miss Bergdorf dress and raincoat in the kitchen of an occupied building trying to figure out how to feed a large number of ravenous postadolescents. The next day I slipped out, went home to change my clothes and slipped back in. Someone put a piece of adhesive on the sleeve of my sweatshirt that read: KITCHEN/COLWIN. This, I feel, marked me for life.

As I began to make what felt like hundreds of peanut butter and jelly sandwiches, my comrades streamed in—Columbia College boys younger than I, and starving.

"Hey! Can I have something to eat?"

"No. We have to save food for mealtimes."

"Hey, I'm starving. Puh-lease?"

"Okay. You can have tuna fish or peanut butter and jelly."

"*Tuna fish! Peanut butter and jelly!* We had peanut butter and jelly for breakfast and I'm allergic to tuna fish."

I learned to say: "Forget it! You're supposed to be eating paving stones like your comrades in Paris." This sent them skulking away. Piles of *The New York Times* showed up mysteriously every morning and we all followed the student strike in Paris as well as the news about ourselves. When people got desperate enough, they either sent runners to Chock Full o' Nuts or implored someone on the street below to provision for them.

One afternoon we dropped a bucket on ropes out of the window, and after lifting it up and down a number of times we had seven dozen eggs. When I went to boil them, I realized that someone had thoughtfully done it for us and we all had boiled eggs for breakfast.

Time has passed and it is fashionable to run down the sixties, but I am proud to have been in that kitchen. The issues were real issues of academic freedom and social justice, about which many students of the time had deep and passionate feelings.

Fourteen years later, I found myself in the kitchen of the Olivieri Center for Homeless Women, on Manhattan's West Side in the heart of the fur district. The Olivieri Center is technically a drop-in center, but women are allowed to sleep there, on the floor. It is two blocks from Pennsylvania Station, seven blocks south of the Port Authority Bus Terminal and across town from Grand Central Station. In all of these places, destitute women live—in the ladies' room, in secret places under the tracks, in the waiting rooms. Many of them find their way to Olivieri, where they can shower, get fresh clothes and eat three meals a day. If they stick around, they can talk to a caseworker who will try to straighten out their entitlements—many women receive supplemental security income, a form of social security for the disabled—or help to get them on public assistance. They can be seen by a doctor and sent to a free clinic.

When I started to volunteer, one hot June morning, the cook, an unflappable, handsome woman named Jean Delmoor, was serving lunch to 120 ladies.

Until you get the notion to volunteer, you do not know who your population is. Some people read to the blind or take deaf children to baseball games. Some people make home visits to the elderly or work with children or runaways. I did not know until I started that my population would be chronically homeless, mentally ill women.

For a couple of months I stayed behind the counter with Jean and performed the services of her sous-chef. I mixed and chopped and fetched and scraped carrots and peeled potatoes. Little by little I got the hang of the place. I got to know the ladies and the ladies began to know me.

None of these women was in very good shape. In addition to schizophrenia, paranoia, psychosis and delusions, these women suffered from diabetes, congestive heart failure and leg ulcerations, the scourge of people who never lie down to sleep. They had neglected teeth, respiratory problems, lice, scabies and TB. There were pregnant women who refused or never received prenatal care. One woman, in fact, delivered on the floor without saying a word. When the caseworker on night duty went to attend to her before the ambulance came, the only words she spoke were: "Do you have a cigarette?"

Some of these women had been homeless for years. Many were former mental patients although there were battered wives, women terrorized out of their Single Room Occupancy hotel rooms by landlords hot to gentrify, mothers burned out of their apartments, or thrown out by boyfriends, husbands and family.

Not one of them was like another. They were and are the most surprising group of people I have ever encountered, and not a single assumption can be made about them except that they are all living in a horrible way. They were old, young and middle-aged. Some women had advanced degrees. Some had hardly finished the fifth grade. They were black, white, Hispanic, of every religion and creed. They came from everywhere on the face of the earth, and one of them was a person who was waiting for a transsexual operation and therefore was not allowed in either the men's or the women's shelter. She or he, wearing mules with pompoms, lived for a while at the Olivieri Center.

But all of them had to be fed and I was happy to be the person ladling lunch onto plates or drawing coffee into Styrofoam cups from a huge urn.

One morning in the fall I turned up and found the kitchen empty.

"Where's Jean?" I asked Juan, who was half security guard and half maintenance man.

"It's her day off," he said.

"Who's cooking?" I asked brightly.

"I guess you," said Juan.

A chill went over my heart.

"How many ladies am I cooking for?"

Juan consulted a sheet.

"About ninety-eight," he said.

I sat down on a milk crate. Suddenly I, who fussed if more than six people came to a dinner party, was responsible for feeding lunch to ninety-eight women.

Downstairs in the pantry were enormous cans of stewed tomatoes, and similarly enormous cans of tomato paste. With Juan to help I brought up onions and spaghetti plus government-surplus Cheddar cheese. In two hours I had made two huge stockpots of tomato sauce and boiled thirty pounds of pasta.

I made my mother's old-fashioned baked spaghetti. The idea is to have much more sauce than pasta and to embed the spaghetti in the sauce. You then bake it in the oven under a thick crust of cheese. I filled four steam-table trays and was vastly relieved to see that it was a hit.

From then on, Jean took her day off on my day on, and I had the kitchen to myself, more or less. I found cooking on Olivieri's six-burner Garland restaurant stove a pleasure, and I spent many waking hours wondering what to make for large numbers of people.

I made chili, baked beans, macaroni and cheese, baked ziti, borscht, cabbage salad, pasta salad, vegetable stew and toasted cheese. One of the ladies' favorite lunches was baked potato, cheese, salad and fruit, a nice lunch for a winter day.

I then got the brilliant idea to make an Irish dish called colcannon, a mixture of spring onions, cabbage and mashed potatoes. The result was not a success, and one of my favorite ladies, who wore fuzzy sweaters, beads, and had a voice like Lauren Bacall's, came up to me and said: "Lunch today, honey. A *disaster*!"

There were ladies who were vegetarians and others furious at not getting meat for lunch. Some women came up and chatted and some never made eye contact. There were ladies who helped peel potatoes and one who washed the pots every day. When I asked her why she did this unrewarding job, she said: "I feel God has been very good to me and I like to pay back."

When I was seven months pregnant, I quit—I could not stand for that long on my feet and I couldn't lift anything heavy.

A few years later my husband and I were being given a tour of the City and Country School, in Greenwich Village. There in the kitchen, I saw a six-burner Garland stove, just like the one at Olivieri. I said to myself: "If our daughter goes to this wonderful school I will certainly end up cooking on this wonderful stove."

A year later, the night before the annual school fair, I was in the kitchen making shepherd's pie for 150 people while two other mothers were making baked ziti (as the vegetarian dish) for another 150. That night, the pasta sauce for the ziti burnt and had to be thrown out. The next day, the man from Con Edison appeared to say that there was a gas leak and that the gas in the entire school was going to be turned off. Meanwhile, it began to rain heavily.

By five o'clock, the gas was back on. We did not have to farm our ziti and shepherd's pie out to ten different households after all. Quantities of delicious tomato sauce had been gotten at an amazing price by a shameless mother who walked into her local Italian cheese store in the pouring rain with her two little children and tears in her eyes. The sky cleared and turned a gorgeous, clear blue. The fair was a huge success and every scrap of food was consumed.

"Isn't cooking for that many kind of nerve-racking?" a friend of mine asked.

But as I was browning thirty-five pounds of meat I realized that I found it extremely relaxing.

SHEPHERD'S PIE

serves 150

10 large onions
4 entire heads of garlic
2-3 cups olive oil
35 pounds chopped chuck
black pepper
2 bottles Worcestershire sauce
10 pounds frozen carrots and peas
1 gallon instant mashed potatoes
fresh grated cheese

1. Have ready four large steam-table trays—these hold around forty portions apiece, more or less.

2. Peel and chop onions and garlic.

3. Heat olive oil in an enormous skillet or low-sided saucepan, and begin to brown some of the meat, adding onions and garlic

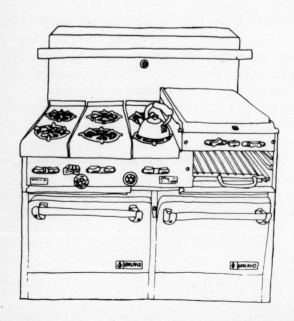

as you go. The browned meat should then be put aside while you brown the rest.

4. Season with black pepper and both bottles of Worcestershire sauce.

5. Apportion the meat into the steam-table trays and add, or rather distribute, previously frozen, now thawed, carrots and peas, and mix well with the meat.

6. Make instant mashed potatoes, stirring with a whisk. Many people find instant potatoes nasty—I do not. You would not want them as a side dish, but on top of a shepherd's pie they are just fine.

7. Spoon a thick layer of potatoes over the meat, sprinkle with fresh grated cheese (not the stuff in jars) and bake in the oven at 300° for two hours.

This will feed 150 people, some of whom are children.

CHOCOLATE

My sister, who is in most other ways a perfectly normal person, is so addicted to chocolate that she routinely compromises her expensive dental work by eating something that I believe is called Rose Shaeffer's Chocolate Lace. This particular confection is made by covering a Jackson Pollock-looking lattice of sticky, filling-and-bridgework-pulling toffee with chocolate. My sister believes that milk chocolate is for twinks and wimps. She eats bittersweet chocolate by the pound and still remains thin.

There are those who must have chocolate and those who can take it or leave it alone. For the afflicted there are magazines devoted to the subject, chocolate cookbooks, candymaker's instruction guides, antique chocolate molds, chocolate dipping courses. There is high-ticket imported chocolate, often in the form of a truffle and often costing only a little less than a real truffle, and novelty chocolate in the form of chocolate arms and legs and telephones. There is weird chocolate, as in chocolate-covered grasshoppers, and then there are candy bars, which those in need of a fix can find almost anywhere.

I like chocolate but I don't love it. I think it is nice every once in a while. I am however a sucker for fudge, which, in my opinion, is chocolate in its most sublime form. On the other hand, I do not like chocolate cake or ice cream and I find the taste of chocolate mixed with liquor just plain awful except in the case of the chocolate-covered cherry, which is the food of my childhood.

In some form or another, chocolate figures in every American's childhood. I remember walking home from school with a candy bar in the days when Three Musketeers really had three pieces. I remember my first taste of Rocky Road ice cream, which my sister adored and I hated. To this day my idea of the perfect dessert is a slightly undercooked chocolate chip cookie made from the recipe on the back of the chocolate morsels' bag. I remember the kind of chocolate pudding that formed a tough skin on the top, and the instant kind that did not.

We did not have chocolate cakes for our birthdays but chocolate played an important role in the cakes we ordered. They were always the same: yellow cake with split layers, the layers alternatingly spread with mocha and apricot jam. The middle layer was marzipan, and the whole thing was covered with bittersweet chocolate icing and decorated with *sugar* roses, not buttercream, because my mother believes that buttercream turns in the hot weather, when all of our birthdays take place. We always found bakers to make this cake, which would have been insipid without that dark, not too sweet icing.

The world is full of chocolate lovers and I have come to rely on three recipes to help those who invite them for dinner: flourless chocolate cake, steamed chocolate pudding and chocolate bread pudding, which when it bubbles over fills the house with what Mary McCarthy describes in *The Groves of Academe* as "a rich smell of burning." The smell of chocolate bubbling over and slightly burning is one of the most beautiful smells in the world. It is subtle and comforting and it *is* rich. One tiny drop perfumes a room as nothing else.

A recipe for a perfect flourless chocolate cake appears in

Elizabeth David's *French Provincial Cooking*. It calls for almonds ground to a powder in the blender, confectioner's sugar, bittersweet chocolate, some very strong coffee, egg yolks and egg whites. It is baked in a springform pan and the egg whites make it rise ever so slightly. As it cools, it slumps. The texture is of the finest fudge or the densest mousse. It is a pure, rich cake with a clear, cooked chocolate taste. All it needs is a little raspberry jam to glaze it and some whipped cream. Ice cream would kill it.

Steamed chocolate pudding is a throwback to a cozier time in American life and is definitely worth making. The 1964 edition of *The Joy of Cooking* has one recipe for it—an elaborate one containing six eggs and nuts, not my idea of a good time. But the 1943 edition (the one with the recipe for gumdrop cookies which begins: "Good for soldiers' boxes as they keep fresh and do not crumble") contains the real winner—a plain, easy and *sincere* steamed pudding, made as follows:

OLD-FASHIONED STEAMED CHOCOLATE PUDDING

serves 4

2 ounces unsweetened chocolate
½ cup sugar
1 egg
1 tablespoon butter, melted and cooled
1 cup all-purpose flour
½ teaspoon baking powder
½ cup milk

1. *Melt chocolate. Let cool.*
2. *Sift sugar.*
3. *Beat egg until light. Add sugar to it gradually and beat until creamy.*

4. Add melted chocolate and then butter.

5. Sift flour. Resift with baking powder. Add to the egg mixture in three parts, alternating the thirds with the milk in three parts. Beat until smooth after each addition.

6. Pour into a buttered pudding mold. Cover with waxed paper tied down with a rubber band and steam in a kettle for one hour.

This pudding tips nicely out of its mold and looks like a baked hat. It is delicious with a raspberry purée, or with whipped cream. Some people like it sliced with a little jam. Steamed puddings have a wonderful satiny texture: half a pudding, half a cake and the nicer half of each.

As for chocolate bread pudding, there is nothing more consoling on a horrible cold night. Any standard cookbook has a recipe for bread pudding, to which you simply add chocolate to the milk and egg. The version I first ate was made of lightly toasted bread spread with sweet butter and set in a dish. The egg, milk and chocolate was poured over it, and the whole thing stood soaking for an hour before baking in a 300° oven for forty-five minutes.

When it comes to chocolate, I prefer the simplest and plainest. To this end I have made chocolate meringues, which must be made when the weather is nice, and chocolate wafers, which taught me a lesson.

These wafers come from *The Settlement Cook Book* by Mrs. Simon Kander (copyright 1926). I have my mother's copy, which is falling to pieces and has written on the endpaper the telephone number for Charlie's vegetable truck service from 1947.

CHOCOLATE WAFERS

2 ounces bitter chocolate
1 cup sugar
½ cup butter, melted
2 eggs
½ cup flour
½ teaspoon vanilla extract

1. Melt chocolate.

2. Add sugar and butter.

3. Add the yolks of eggs into the beaten egg whites and stir into the chocolate mixture.

4. Add flour and vanilla.

5. Spread on a well-buttered pan. Place in a 350° oven but gradually decrease the heat to 300°.

6. This recipe does not tell you how long to bake. I would say about ten to twelve minutes. Cut into squares while still warm.

I made these cookies to serve with a fruit salad one spring night and was alarmed at how tasteless they were. No one liked them very much but I could not bear to throw them out, so I put them in a tin and left them for a couple of days. One afternoon when my blood sugar dropped and it was time for tea, I remembered the chocolate wafers. "Better than nothing," I said to myself, biting into one. To my amazement, they were delicious. They tasted strongly and wonderfully of chocolate and were hard and crunchy, too. It had taken a couple of days for the taste to bloom and it was worth the wait. And so I add to Mrs. Simon Kander's admirable recipe a seventh step:

7. Let cool, put in a tin and do not eat for at least *two days.*

And of course, for those of you about to give a dinner party for chocolate nuts, you know what bakeries are for: so that, at the end of dinner, you can put your feet up and have the chocolate dessert you didn't bake.

THE SAME OLD THING

Many of my closest friends are sick of my baked chicken, and even when I point out that I know a million variations on this theme, they rightly point out that they have had them all, and more than once.

But when the chips are down, the spirit is exhausted and the body hungry, the same old thing is a great consolation. When people who must provide meals are too tired to think of what to cook, those old standbys come to the rescue. These are things a person can cook half asleep.

For instance, frittata. Even on a Sunday night, a little butter and some olive oil can be found in most households, and usually some eggs. A frittata is a flat Italian omelet that can be eaten hot or cold and the ingredients are limitless. A mushroom and zucchini frittata is nice, and so is a red pepper and onion frittata, but suppose you have no peppers or mushrooms? The answer is potato frittata, which tastes good and is handy since people tend to *store* potatoes.

For two people you need one large potato cut into dice, four eggs and some minced garlic. The potatoes are sautéed with garlic in olive oil or butter, and when they are cooked, the scrambled eggs are slipped in and left to cook gently. Frittata should be cooked in a metal-handled skillet since you may want to stick it under the broiler for a minute or two (perhaps with a dusting of grated cheese) to brown the top. Even a child will eat it, and with a green salad and something nice for dessert, it makes a meal.

For more years than I like to think about, a variation on baked chicken was my party standby, and with it I always served the same old thing: creamed spinach with jalapeño peppers. I could not get enough, as the song says, of this wonderful stuff. My friends liked it too, and I was happy to pass the recipe along. My friends fed it to their friends, and so on. By now, probably half the people in the Western Hemisphere have eaten this savory dish.

One November, at a literary festival in Dallas, Texas, I and the other participants were fed a delicious meal in a beautiful house. The side dish was creamed spinach with jalapeño peppers and it was so good it made me want to sit up and beg like a dog. Without a trace of shame I marched up to the hostess and pleaded for the recipe. This nice woman presented me, shortly thereafter, with a green card which read FROM THE KITCHEN OF BETTY JOSEY and there was the recipe, which I have altered just a little (since it is hard to find jalapeño cheese up north):

CREAMED SPINACH WITH JALAPEÑO PEPPERS

serves 4-6

2 packages frozen spinach
4 tablespoons butter
2 tablespoons flour
2 tablespoons onion, chopped
1 clove garlic, minced
½ cup evaporated milk

½ teaspoon black pepper
¾ teaspoon celery salt
6 ounces Monterey Jack cheese, cubed
1 or more jalapeño peppers, chopped
buttered bread crumbs

1. Cook spinach. Drain, reserving one cup of liquid, and chop fine.

2. Melt butter in a saucepan and add flour. Blend and cook a little. Do not brown.

3. Add onion and garlic.

4. Add one cup of spinach liquid slowly, then add evaporated milk, some fresh black pepper, celery salt and cheese. Add one or more chopped jalapeño pepper (how many is a question of taste as well as what kind. I myself use the pickled kind, from a jar) and then the spinach. Cook until all is blended.

5. Turn into a buttered casserole topped with buttered bread crumbs and bake for about forty-five minutes at 300°.

After about five hundred or so casseroles of creamed spinach with jalapeño peppers, I felt it was time to move on to a new side dish. For a while I was stuck on baked polenta with cheese, but eventually I settled down with orzo.

Orzo is a rice-shaped pasta which can sometimes be found in the spaghetti section of a supermarket, and can always be found in Greek or Italian specialty stores. I am not much of a rice cook, although I have tried and tried. I have sautéed the rice first, put tea towels under the lid, steamed it in the oven, but I never get it right. Orzo, on the other hand, never fails.

Orzo with butter and grated cheese is very nice. Orzo with a little ricotta, some chopped parsley and scallion, butter and cheese, is even better. Orzo with chopped broccoli and broccoli di rape is heaven, and it is also a snap. While you cook the orzo, steam the two broccolis—the amounts depend entirely on how many people you are feeding—until tender. Chop and set aside.

Drain the orzo and throw in a lump of butter. Stir it in, add the broccoli, some fresh black pepper and some grated cheese, and you have a side dish fit for a visiting dignitary from a country whose politics you admire.

This certainly was good for a few hundred parties, but people, unlike other mammals, tend to get bored. Eventually I began to hear faint protests (especially since the orzo was so frequently served with chicken), and I knew I had to expand my repertoire.

For a while I turned to meat loaf. I myself love meat loaf and find even ones that have been lying around on a steam table palatable. I especially adore a meat loaf sandwich, but as we know, you can't have a meat loaf sandwich without making a meat loaf.

Meat loaf ranges from the sublime (the one in Marcella Hazan's first volume that contains funghi porcini and is cooked in white wine) to the pedestrian: meat, egg, seasoning and bread crumbs. Meat loaf is not usually a party dish but one day I decided that I would make a meat loaf with a design in it, to resemble the gorgeous torta rustica I had seen in a fancy Italian restaurant.

I packed half the seasoned meat into a loaf pan. Then I added a layer of spinach chopped up fine with scallions. On top of this I placed three hard-boiled eggs, shelled and wrapped in pimiento. Then I covered them with the rest of the meat and put it in the oven. When it was done, I left it to cool and then put it in the refrigerator for an hour or so to set.

When sliced, the result looked like sunset over the Mediterranean and was much admired, except that it was plain old meat loaf and everyone knew it.

One of my most popular fallback recipes is for something called vegetable fritters. These are not fritters, properly so-called, but they are made of vegetables. They are really little potato croquettes made with chopped-up vegetables.

The base of vegetable fritters is mashed potatoes to which you add one beaten egg. I like to add pepper and minced garlic. To this you add the leftover brussels sprouts or broccoli chopped up fine, a little finely diced carrot, some bean sprouts for crunch, scallions, onions—anything you have around. Form into cakes, roll in fine bread crumbs and fry in butter or olive oil or light sesame oil. Serve with either homemade tomato sauce, salsa or plain old catsup. These are a hit with children, who use them as a vehicle for the catsup, but adults like them, too. Furthermore, they are easy, filling, tasty and they are also good for you.

Two winters ago, when our boiler shut down during a spell of arctic air in January, I discovered something that became a standby at once. To keep the oven on, I decided to make baked beans, which would keep the kitchen warm overnight.

For baked beans I like to use little white beans, sometimes called Yankee, sometimes called navy and sometimes just called little white beans. They are cooked with an onion and two cloves of garlic, a bay leaf and some black pepper until just tender enough so that you can blow the skin off.

I have a bean pot that has no top, and as I put the beans in I realized I was going to have to invent one, but first I seasoned the beans.

Many people like to put a chunk of double-smoked bacon in with their beans but some people do not. I omitted the bacon and made a sauce of tomato paste, tomato sauce, molasses, Worcestershire sauce and Dijon mustard. This sauce must be made according to taste. Some people like their beans sweet, some savory. The proportions are entirely up to the cook and the amount depends upon the amount of beans.

Then I made a dough of flour and water, kneaded it and rolled it out until it was wide enough to make a lid for the bean pot and seal up the sides. I put the whole thing in the oven at 250° before refilling the hot water bottles, stoking the fire and checking all the space heaters.

The next morning I removed the bean pot and there on the top was a beautiful dark brown lid that came off in one piece to the delight of my then two-year-old daughter. The oven had kept the kitchen warm but there was no delicious smell of baked beans since the lid really was airtight. The beans were rich and savory and had the most wonderful texture: firm but tender. They had been gently steamed but had not gotten mushy.

By the time the heat came back on I decided I would make real Boston brown bread. I have now made this so many times I could make it under general anesthesia. If you make it you will come to know why generations of Bostonians lived on this perfect combination. I make it in an ornamental pudding mold but a pudding basin or Pyrex bowl will do as well.

REAL BOSTON BROWN BREAD

1 cup stone-ground yellow or white cornmeal
1 cup rye flour
1 cup whole-wheat flour
¾ teaspoon baking soda
1 teaspoon salt
2 cups low-fat buttermilk
(or milk mixed half and half with yogurt)
¾ cup molasses
1-1½ cups raisins

1. Combine cornmeal, rye flour and whole-wheat flour with baking soda and salt.

2. In another bowl combine low-fat buttermilk (or milk-yogurt mixture), molasses and raisins.

3. Add the liquids to the dry ingredients and turn into a very lavishly buttered six-cup mold. Fill three-quarters full, leaving room for the bread to expand.

4. Cover with pleated waxed paper (which will expand as the bread rises) and tie down with a rubber band.

5. Place the mold in a kettle of hot water to come three-quarters of the way up the mold. Bring to a boil, slow down to a simmer. Cover and steam for three and a half hours, checking every once in a while to make sure the water level stays at three-quarters.

Unmolded, this is a beautiful thing. You can feed it to anyone. It can be eaten with butter and jam, or with cream cheese or with nothing at all. It will keep you going through the winter and by the time everyone is sick of it, it will be spring. By late fall you will be getting requests for it again.

And just as you are ready to branch out to, say, carbonnade à la flamande (beef braised in beer—good for at least seventy dinner parties) someone is sure to say: "Why don't you make that nice baked chicken anymore?"

And there you have it. The same old thing never goes out of fashion.

RED PEPPERS

A raw red pepper is a nice enough vegetable—crunchy and slightly sweet—but roasted or sautéed in olive oil, the red pepper takes on depth. It becomes soft and intense with a smooth, smoky aftertaste. I have been addicted to paprika—red pepper in its powdered form—all my life and I would not dream of cooking without it.

I have always believed that if you listen to your food cravings (I do not mean your constant desire for chocolate brownies) they will tell you what you need. If you long for bananas, it may be potassium you need. I myself once experienced a craving for red peppers so intense that I bought a large bag of them and ate them all as I walked home. Peppers contain large quantities of vitamin A and lesser amounts of vitamin C, as well as phosphorus and iron, but what the hell? As a doctor friend of mine once said, it is silly to do anything for reasons of health. My body may have been crying out for vitamins, but my spirit wanted red peppers.

Autumn is red pepper season and the tables of farmers' markets are heaped with them. The best are on the long and skinny (as opposed to round and short) side, and the flesh is thin. The redder the better is my motto, but after peppers ripen, they have to be watched closely and used quickly or they develop unhappy-looking soft patches, and eventually they rot.

A large number of red peppers is a beautiful sight. Even more beautiful is the sight of them cut into strips and ready to be simmered in a large pot of fruity olive oil. And of course, most magnificent of all is a large glass jar packed with fried peppers, studded with slivered garlic cloves, seasoned with salt, pepper, the juice of half a lemon and covered with the olive oil they were fried in. Some people might call this Red Pepper Conserve, but it will always be red pepper sludge to me.

This yummy condiment can be used to create a pasta sauce, or served with mozzarella cheese, or put on egg salad or a hero sandwich, or spread on Italian bread as an hors d'oeuvre. I confess that I have been known to stand over the jar with a long fork and simply eat the contents by themselves.

In the fall you can often get black and yellow peppers which, along with red and green, look beautiful in a jar to give away to a friend—if you can bear to part with it.

Anyone who has ever been to an Italian restaurant knows that red peppers and anchovies were made for each other and thus this combination appears on a thousand menus. Red peppers sometimes turn up instead of green for stuffed peppers, or they show up in a salad. For most people, that does it for red peppers, but for addicts, enough is never enough.

I love red peppers fried in olive oil more than almost anything else, but I am often alone in this adoration. Frequently people want a little something else with their peppers. For them:

WARM POTATO SALAD
WITH FRIED RED PEPPERS

serves 4-6

8 medium red potatoes
3 red peppers
½ cup olive oil
2 cloves garlic, cut on diagonal
black pepper
juice of one lemon
salt

1. Boil potatoes.
2. Cut peppers into strips and fry gently in olive oil, along with a few pieces of garlic. Add a few grinds of fresh black pepper.
3. Cut the warm, cooked potatoes into chunks; add the peppers, garlic and olive oil. Sprinkle with lemon juice and salt and serve warm.

Baked vegetables are a wonderful thing, and always include peppers. Peppers of as many colors as you can get, onions, and large, waxy potatoes cut into rounds cook deliciously in a big roasting pan in a dousing of olive oil and pepper. This dish can be eaten hot, cold or lukewarm and is perfect in any season: with cold roast chicken in the summer, with a frittata in the spring, with a pot roast in the winter, and with little quails in the fall.

But somewhere there are people who do not like olive oil and for them, pimientos are the answer. These are easy to prepare and interesting to young children. Roast the pepper over the gas burner on a skewer or long fork. The skin of the pepper will char and turn black. This is always quite fascinating to watch. Turn the pepper until it is burnt all over and then rinse off the charred skin under cold water. This roasting cooks the pepper and gives it a silky texture. At the same time it brings out its smoky taste. Pimientos can be eaten as is, with salt and pepper, or chopped up in a sandwich, or made into a savory sandwich spread that calls for chopped pimiento, an equal amount of sharp Cheddar cheese chopped fine, a pinch of pepper and a binding of mayonnaise.

A long time ago I fell in love with a dish called Pepper Zucchini served at a restaurant on the upper East Side of Manhattan called the Café Divino. Since I do not live on the upper East Side and therefore could not go to the Café Divino every day, I was forced to try to replicate this dish in my own insufficient kitchen.

PEPPER ZUCCHINI

serves 2-4

pimientos from 2 red peppers (see p. 90)
4 small, young zucchini
flour
olive oil
three cloves garlic, slivered
salt and pepper
lemon juice

1. Cut pimientos in flat pieces and set aside.
2. Cut zucchini into slices—not too thick or thin—lengthwise and dust with flour. Fry gently in olive oil. They should be cooked on both sides, and when they are just beginning to get a little crisp on one side, they are done. Arrange them on a plate.
3. Place the pimiento on the zucchini. Strain the olive oil and sprinkle on top. Add garlic but remove before serving. Sprinkle with salt, pepper and lemon juice.

This is one of the nicest things you will ever eat, and it is good for you, too.

Some years ago at a dinner party I was served a braised loin of pork with vegetables. As good as it was, the vegetables were much more delectable than the meat.

BRAISED FENNEL, CELERY, ONION AND RED PEPPER

serves 2-4

1 bunch celery
1 head fennel
2 big yellow onions
2 red peppers
2 oz. butter
½ lemon
¼-½ cup chicken stock
salt and pepper

1. Use the bottom part—the heart—of the celery; celery root will not do for this dish. Cut celery into four pieces lengthwise.
2. Trim fennel and cut into four pieces lengthwise.
3. Cut onions into four pieces lengthwise.
4. Cut peppers into large strips.
5. Nestle these vegetables together in an ovenproof dish with a lid. Dot with butter. Add lemon juice and some chicken stock (this can be omitted if you are a vegetarian).
6. Add salt and fresh pepper.
7. Bake in a moderate oven for about forty minutes.

It is clear that I have come a long way from the days when I would eat a bag of peppers on the street, but considering that I can eat a mess of them straight from the frying pan, perhaps I haven't come that far after all.

DINNER PARTIES

It is a fact of life that people give dinner parties, and when they invite you, you have to turn around and invite them back. Often they retaliate by inviting you again, and you must then extend another invitation. Back and forth you go, like Ping-Pong balls, and what you end up with is called social life.

Of course, one person's dinner party is another's potluck supper. Glossy photos in magazines of women wearing eight-thousand-dollar dresses lighting huge numbers of candles in huge numbers of Georgian silver candlesticks on a table that seats forty can be pretty depressing when all you have is a ratty sweater and an old dishwasher. In the photos liveried footmen hover in the background hiding a battalion of cooks and cleaners. To the average person, the dishwasher stands in for any number of servants. Of course, some people actually have a servant who takes away the plates after each course and then brings new, clean ones. In other households, this person is often called a husband.

In the old days, women planned dinner parties by sitting

down with the cook and discussing what might be nice to serve. The cook or the cook's servant did the shopping. The table was set by the scullery maid. The hostess's job was to dress well and smile, and the husband poured the wine. Then, while the men smoked cigars in one room, and the women gossiped in another, the table was magically cleared and everything was washed and put away.

Nowadays, almost everyone works and the hostess usually spends a few days on and off consulting with the cook, a replica of the hostess, at about two o'clock in the morning when she can't sleep. The cook's servant, another twin to the hostess, does the shopping on the way to or on the way home from work, and the butler, a double of the husband, buys the wine and some flowers. The cook and butler rush home, set the table, start the meal, and just as they collapse exhausted in their chairs with a glass of wine, the guests arrive.

Some people like to feed lots of people at a time. Often this pays back several invitations at once. Others like to mix and match their friends. I know a couple who keep a kind of dinner party log: who came, who was matched with whom and what was served. I myself feel that eight for dinner without help makes the host and hostess jumpy. Six creates fewer dishes and less din.

But what to feed them? The idea of a dinner party is rather like the idea of a novel. People who have never written novels say: "Oh, but they're so long and have so many chapters!" Many people feel just that way about dinner parties: "They're so long and have so many courses!" Just as novels are written chapter by chapter, so are dinner parties put together course by course. And just as novels are not necessarily written from beginning to middle to end (although they end up that way), it is easier to think about a dinner party course by course, but not consecutively.

The easiest thing to think about is salad. Salad, as a course by itself, requires almost nothing. A bunch of watercress, a few scallions is all it takes, plus olive oil, salt, pepper and vinegar or lemon juice. A dressing can be mixed beforehand: this takes about five seconds; or the salad can be dressed at the table, which also takes about five seconds. Bread and cheese are often served with the salad course, both of which can be bought. This requires nothing more of the cook than some cash and a trip to a nice cheese store.

Dessert can also be bought if you are exhausted and not inclined to dessert making. But to some, dessert is the fun part, both in the cooking and the eating. Millions of delicious things can be made in advance.

That takes care of two whole courses, leaving a main course, a first course and hors d'oeuvres.

Because I am always hungry, I myself eschew hors d'oeuvres. When they come my way, I eat too many and then am full by the time I reach the table. This does not, however, prevent me from cleaning my plate and then I am angry at myself for eating too much.

Hors d'oeuvres were invented to eat with drinks, a long time before a meal. Often, people make a meal of them. Since people are bound to sit around talking and drinking before sitting down to dinner, you must give them something to nibble on. Salted nuts, olives or cheese straws are quite sufficient. If you happen not to have any of these things, French bread cut into rounds, brushed with olive oil and dusted with Parmesan cheese and toasted in the oven is quick and good.

Some diehards feel that to give a dinner party without a starter is barbaric. Mellower types want to get right down to the good stuff and not mess around with some funny little thing on a small plate. Some hosts and hostesses are too tired to worry about a first and a second course and wish they had called the whole thing off.

A first course can always be bought—for example, smoked salmon, or sliced cucumbers with a spicy dressing are extremely simple and cost next to nothing. Some people serve a vegetable as a starter, such as blanched asparagus or grilled eggplant. In the summer, sliced tomatoes with olive oil and basil make a perfect, effortless starter but this will not satisfy the ambitious who like to produce spinach soufflés and creamed soups. A great aid to the first course is the blender, in which, if you combine yogurt, chicken stock, peeled cucumbers and a little cracked wheat and lemon juice, you can make soup in less than ten seconds.

This leaves the main course to worry about. In the old days, it was just the other way around. Everyone knew what to serve for dinner: leg of lamb. It was all those other things that complicated a meal. Leg of lamb, beloved by hostesses of previous generations, is one of the easiest things to render inedible. Often leathery slices of gray cardboard or quivering pieces of red matting with the texture of wet socks were offered to dinner guests. Lamb must be *pink*. Rare lamb, so popular these days, is simply disgusting and should never be eaten. But it is hard to get a leg of lamb right and it is relieving to see that it has gone out of fashion. Also out of fashion, like the boxer dog and the poodle skirt, is roast beef, since people who will eat an entire strawberry shortcake feel funny about red meat and fat, or feel they cannot buy standing ribs for six and have anything left over for, say, school tuition or the dry cleaner.

Potential hosts and hostesses can learn much as guests in the homes of others. From the position of invited victim, I have learned that it is unwise to produce an exotic meal, especially one you have never made before, for a dinner party. I remember with a dread clarity a dinner party with a long drinks period. When every scrap of cheese, olive, and stick of celery had been devoured, we were called, still ravenous, to the table. Once we were seated, the hostess appeared bearing a large pumpkin. This puzzled us all.

"What's *that*?" said a rude guest.

"It's an Argentine dish!" our friend said cheerily. At these words I felt a little snake of unhappy anticipation crawl up my neck.

From the bowels of this pumpkin came forth a strange substance that was neither soup nor stew and contained overcooked meat and undercooked eggplant. I wondered how this had been done and realized the meat and eggplant had been cooked separately. We sat at an enormous table and drank a vast quantity of expensive wine. Later I peeked into the huge and luxurious kitchen that had produced this unusually awful meal.

I also remember a dinner party for six given in an overheated little box of an apartment with one window over an airshaft. This was the first New York apartment of a young Englishwoman who was a demon party giver and one of the finest cooks I have ever known. She was not about to let her nasty and tiny kitchen get in the way of her good time. She gave us curried parsnip soup, roast loin of pork, a delicious salad and chocolate bread pudding for dessert, leaving her guests weak with gratitude and longing to sit in big chairs to savor our coffee, but that little flat had only one chair except for the borrowed camp chairs at her makeshift table.

Soon after that she moved to a slightly larger apartment with two windows, where she often fed fifteen people five courses.

But this young woman is an extreme type—a wonderful cook who adores entertaining above all else. Others are lazier, not as accomplished and often not so friendly. For them it is wise to have a no-fail dinner party menu that can be counted on to make people happy and not leave the hostess in a state of hysteria.

For several years I caused my friends to be intimate with one of two meals: chili, potato salad, shortbread and ice cream for dessert, or baked mustard chicken, potato salad, creamed spinach with jalapeño peppers, shortbread and ice cream for dessert.

Any basic cookbook has a recipe for shortbread—butter, sugar and flour and almost no one makes it anymore. With ice cream it is sublime—a true no-hassle dessert.

The chicken is cut up and coated with mustard into which some garlic has been grated, along with a little thyme, black pepper and a pinch of cinnamon. It is rolled in fine bread crumbs, dusted with paprika, dotted with butter and cooked at 350° for about two hours. It can be served hot or at room temperature and will never let you down.

The potato salad contains potatoes, scallions, black pepper and mayonnaise thinned with lemon juice.

After you have cooked your party dinner six or seven times, you will be able to do it in your sleep, but your friends will be bored. You will then have to go in search of new friends who have never had creamed spinach with jalapeño peppers, or you will have to find something new to feed your old friends. In either case, you will be helping to keep the wheels of society spinning in an effortless and graceful way, and no one will ever know how antisocial you really are.

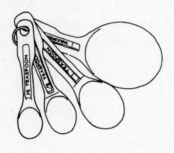

HOW TO AVOID GRILLING

U nlike most citizens of these United States of America, I do not grill. There is no hibachi in my garden or anything else like it. When I moved into my garden apartment I was given a fancy barbecue, and as far as I know it is still in the cellar collecting dust and mold spores.

Grilling is like sunbathing. Everyone knows it is bad for you but no one ever stops doing it. Since I do not like the taste of lighter fluid, I do not have to worry that a grilled steak is the equivalent of seven hundred cigarettes.

Of course this implies that I do not like to eat al fresco. No sane person does, I feel. When it is nice enough for people to eat outside, it is also nice enough for mosquitoes, horse and deer flies, as well as wasps and yellowjackets. I don't much like sand in my food and thus while I will endure a beach picnic I never look forward to them.

My idea of bliss is a screened-in porch from which you can watch the sun go down, or come up. You can sit in temperate shade and not fry your brains while you eat. You are protected from flying critters, sandstorms and rain and you can still enjoy a nice cool breeze.

One year my husband and I rented a lake cottage—a rustic cabin set in a pine grove just a stroll from a weed-choked lake. With this cottage came a war canoe and a screened-in porch. The motto of the owners seemed to have been: "It's broken! Let's take it to the lake!"

The dining room table was on a definite slant and the plates were vintage 1950s Melmac. The stove was lit by one of those gizmos that ignite a spark next to one of the burners and was of great fascination to me. Near the corner cupboards lived an army of mice who left evidence of their existence all over the cups and saucers. Anything left around was carried away—quite a tidy little ecosystem. One evening we were visited by a dog who howled constantly as the sound of mouse rattling drove him into a frenzy.

Nevertheless, we ate on the screened-in porch all the time and with great success. Friends with beautiful houses came to our broken-down lake cottage to eat on that crummy porch and watch the sun set over the lake. All around us were grills: we could smell them, but we never so much as fingered a charcoal briquette.

Having said this, I admit to loving grilled food—that is, something that has been exposed to a flame. On a regular old stove this is called broiling. English stoves have a special rack (a salamander) with a separate flame under which you can grill a chop or brown the top of a gratin. There is no better way to cook fish, steak or chops.

I have avoided grilling by broiling, and I have never had to bother myself about getting in a supply of mesquite or apple wood, or old thyme twigs.

For a brief period of my life I thought to use the fireplace as a cooking surface. Years of ingesting gasoline at the barbecues of others led me to wonder if I could do it better. I decided to grill steaks on a rack in my fireplace and by a stroke of fortune was given some apple and cherry to burn. The results were marred by nervousness, a syndrome that goes with the territory of the wood fire: constant cutting to see how far along your steak has come. I did not taste the merest breath of apple or cherry although I have been told that you have not lived until you have tasted swordfish grilled over mesquite. This may be true, but as Abraham Lincoln is said to have said: "For people who like this sort of thing, this is the sort of thing they will like."

But what to do on a clear summer evening? The sky is pink. The air is sweet. It is dinnertime and you are surrounded by hungry people who have just spent the day either swimming or gardening, or have just gotten out of a car or train or bus and found themselves in the country listening to the hermit thrushes.

Everywhere in America people are lighting their grills. They begin in spring, on the first balmy evening. I happen to live across the street from a theological seminary whose students come from all over. I know it is spring not by the first robin but by the first barbecue across the street on the seminary lawn. That first whiff of lighter fluid and smoke is my herald, and led one of my friends to ask: "What is it about Episcopalians, do you think? Is it in their genes to barbecue?"

It is not in the genes but it is in the American character to grill, a leftover from pioneer days, from Indian days, from the Old West. I have been able to buck this trend with Lebanon bologna sandwiches or mustard chicken.

Lebanon bologna is not from the Middle East but from Lebanon, Pennsylvania, in Lancaster County. It is a spicy, slightly tart salami-like cold cut with the limpness of bologna. I have never had the courage to ask what it is made of but I am sure it cannot be good for anyone. The way to serve it is on whole-wheat bread spread with cream cheese into which you have mashed chives, thyme, tarragon—whatever you or your friends have in the garden. Spread the cream cheese liberally but use only one (two if sliced very thin) slice of Lebanon bologna. Make an enormous pile of these sandwiches cut in half and serve with potato salad, cole slaw or a big green salad. In the summer a large plate of sliced tomatoes is a salad in itself with nothing added.

If you feel you must make something more grill-like, spare ribs are always nice, especially if you have marinated them for a couple of days.

Some people like a tomato-based barbecue sauce, but I do not. Besides, these ribs are baked in the oven, not barbecued. I like them in what is probably a variation on teriyaki sauce.

For one side of ribs you need one cup of olive oil, one half cup tamari sauce, about four tablespoons of honey, the juice of one lemon, fresh ground black pepper and lots and lots and lots of garlic peeled and cut in half. Let the ribs sit in this marinade as long as possible—overnight in the refrigerator is the least, two days is the best. Then put the ribs in a roasting pan (you can either cut them into riblets or leave them in one piece and cut before serving) and put them in a slow oven—about 300°—and leave them there, pouring off the fat from time to time, for three to four hours. What is left, as a friend of mine says, has no name. The ribs are both crisp and tender, salty, sweet, oily but not greasy and very garlicky. You gnaw on them and then throw the bones on the platter.

A finger bowl is actually appropriate here, if you want to be fancy, and so is the kind of heated washcloth you get in a Japanese restaurant. Plain old wet paper towels will do as well.

You can cook these ribs in the morning and eat them in the evening. They should not be cold (although a leftover rib for breakfast is considered heavenly by some people) but are fine lukewarm, and can be kept in a warm oven with no ill effects.

And as the sky becomes overcast and the clouds get darker, and the fumes of charcoal starter drift in your direction, you can sit down to your already cooked dinner in a safe place with the satisfaction of not having had to light a single match or get your hands all gritty with those nasty, smeary little charcoal bri-quettes. Furthermore, you will never in your life have to clean the grill, one of the most loathsome of kitchen chores.

Instead you are indoors while being out of doors. Your dinner is taken care of and you can concentrate on eating, which, after a long summer day, is all anybody really wants.

NURSERY FOOD

A long time ago it occurred to me that when people are tired and hungry, which in adult life is much of the time, they do not want to be confronted by an intellectually challenging meal: they want to be consoled.

When life is hard and the day has been long, the ideal dinner is not four perfect courses, each in a lovely pool of sauce whose ambrosial flavors are like nothing ever before tasted, but rather something comforting and savory, easy on the digestion— something that makes one feel, if even for only a minute, that one is safe. A four-star meal is the right thing when the human animal is well rested and feeling rich, but it is not much help to the sore in spirit who would be much better off with a big bowl of homemade soup.

Once upon a time when I was in mourning for my father I was taken home by my best friend who sat me in a chair, gave me a copy of *Vogue* and told me not to move until called. I sat like a good girl while she busied herself in the kitchen. When I got to the table I realized that this angelic pal had made shepherd's pie. My eyes swam with tears of gratitude. I did not know that shepherd's pie was just what I wanted, but it was just what I wanted.

Of course I do not mean that you should feed your friends pastina and beef tea (although I would be glad to be served either). But dishes such as shepherd's pie and chicken soup are a kind of edible therapy. After a good nursery dinner you want your guests to smile happily and say with childlike contentment: "I haven't had that in *years*."

I have managed to stretch the term nursery food like Silly Putty, and under its pliant heading comes a wide variety of dishes: fried chicken, lamb stew, macaroni and cheese, meatballs, baked beans, lentil soup, chili, baked stuffed potatoes, and lasagna. This is rounded out by an adult salad: there is no such thing as nursery salad. For dessert, lemon fluff, shortbread, custard, bread pudding, apple crisp, steamed chocolate pudding or ginger cake.

These are the sorts of things you never see on restaurant menus unless you are lucky enough to find one of those few surviving ladies' tearooms. Nowadays you won't even find dishes like these served to you at other people's houses, unless they have small children and you are not above stealing food off a baby's plate. This is the age of competitive cookery, and therefore when invited to a dinner party you are more than likely to get salmon medallions in sorrel sauce and caviar, or sautéed lobster with champagne, salads made with walnut oil, and cakes that look intimidatingly professional. Meals like this are swell, but they are not true home meals.

Nursery food borrows nicely from other cuisines. The spinach and lamb found on Indian menus as *saag mhaan* makes a perfect nursery dish, for instance. Minorcan potatoes—a layer of potatoes, a layer of tomatoes, plenty of garlic, bread crumbs and olive oil, baked—is nursery food for older people. But *cassoulet* is not. It has too many ingredients that are weird, such as *confit d'oie*, or that are hard to digest, such as *saucisson*.

Many people believe that the essence of nursery food is that it can be mashed up with a fork and that it does not require much in the way of chewing. Parts of a nursery dinner should be eaten without any utensils at all: corn sticks, cookies, steamed carrots and baby lamb chops, for example. You will never, never hear your guests say the words no host or hostess ever, ever wants to hear: "That was interesting. What *was* it?"

In this uncertain world of ours the thing about nursery food is that you can count on it. You know what it is. It will not give you any nasty surprises. ("No darling, that was raw tuna, not marinated Indonesian beef.") It leaves you neither guessing nor lost in admiration. It fills, cheers and makes you feel it ought to be eaten from one of those metal-bottomed hot-water baby dishes with three little china sections and a picture of the gingham dog and the calico cat in each.

And though I would never turn down a four-star meal (or even a two- or three- one) at some fancy place, on a cold night after a hard day I would reverse my steps if someone offered me a homemade vegetable fritter with catsup, Welsh rabbit or some real creamed spinach.

The ultimate nursery food is beef tea; I have not had it since I was a child, and although I could easily have brewed myself a batch, I never have yet. I am afraid that my childhood will overwhelm me with the first sip or that I will be compelled to sit down at once and write a novel in many volumes. I am not afraid it will not be as delicious as I remember it. It will. Now that I have a child of my own I know the day is coming when I will make beef tea for her, and I am certainly not above insisting that she share it with her mother.

It is made as follows, according to my mother:

You take one pound of absolutely fatless silver tip of beef and on a doubled sheet of butcher paper or a wood board cut it into tiny dice. Place it and any juices the meat has yielded in the top of a double boiler and gently cook, covered, over simmering water for several hours. Do not use salt or pepper. Simply leave the meat alone to give off its juices. After several hours you will be left with pure essence of beef, perfectly digestible and nourishing. Strain into a warm bowl, then press out any additional juice from the meat. The meat itself is useless, a mere net of fibers, and should be given to the dog.

Beef tea can be eaten by the very delicate from a spoon. In my family, not known for the delicacy with which food is approached, we drank it by the glass. It is recommended for frazzled adults and children recovering from minor ailments.

More substantial and less digestible a form of nursery food is baked eggs, a staple of my childhood. The proper vessel to cook them in is a small covered Pyrex dish. An earthenware dish will do, except that you can't see through it to see if the eggs are done.

The Pyrex dish is put in the oven to hotten up. When hot, a

lump of butter the size of a walnut (as the old cookbooks say) is dropped in to melt. When the butter is just slightly sizzling, break in the eggs, never more than four. Sprinkle with black pepper and Parmesan but no salt, as the Parmesan is salty enough. Cover and bake in a 325° oven until done. Done can mean just cooked, or pink around the edges of the yolks, or baked to the consistency of a rubber eraser—some children like eggs this way. Baked eggs, though, have to be watched.

The perfect accompaniment is a tomato salad or a side dish of pickled beets. This makes a lovely dinner for a cool summer night: easy to make and quick to cook, a good thing to keep in mind when people are starving and no one feels much like fussing.

In a perfect world, baked eggs are served on a plate that has the letters of the alphabet around the rim and a picture of a clown jumping over the letter X. As a side dish, buttered white toast cut up to postage-stamp size is just right, with a large glass of milk—perhaps in a jelly glass—or a cup of cocoa.

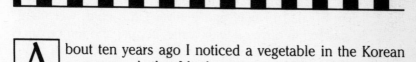

BITTER GREENS

About ten years ago I noticed a vegetable in the Korean greengrocer's that I had never seen before. It was leafy, stalky and had little broccoli-like florets on the end, some of which sprouted tiny yellow flowers. I was told that this was bitter broccoli.

I saw it again in an Italian market. This time it was called broccoli di rape. In its next incarnation it was broccoli rabe, and then I found it in a seed catalogue classified as rapini.

Finally, I decided to try it. I steamed it, served it with butter and everyone hated it. Something told me, however, that this was my fault and not the fault of broccoli di rape.

I took a flyer on it in an Italian restaurant where it had been cooked until very tender in chicken stock with garlic and was served with grated cheese. Since then, I have never looked back.

I bought another bunch, trimmed and steamed it until it was tender, sautéed it in olive oil and garlic. The next bunch I ate cold with vinaigrette. Eventually when I found myself eating it right out of the steamer I realized I was addicted to it.

"Don't serve it to men," said an English friend of mine who is a demon cook. "Men don't like bitter greens."

It seems she had had a sad experience with some fellow and an endive or chicory salad. And it was certainly true that my husband was not mad keen for broccoli di rape.

This green, which is not in the broccoli family at all but is a form of Italian mustard, appears in the markets in September and begins to fade away in April. It is not so much bitter as pungent, although it *is* slightly bitter. This makes it a perfect foil for spicy or buttery food. Naturally, it is very good for people if you can find a way to get them to eat it.

Broccoli di rape is my favorite amongst bitter greens, but I am also fond of chicory, endive and escarole. These I serve once in a while. After a savory dish such as chili con queso or eggplant parmigiana or lasagna, I like to serve a chicory salad. With duck, I like a salad of beet and endive. On a cold, wet night, escarole sautéed in olive oil with garlic, pepper and lemon juice is just the thing. But nothing comes close to broccoli di rape, which I could eat happily every day of the week and never tire of.

Since it is definitely an adult taste, it is best to serve it to adults. A good bunch is one with more buds than leaves. There should not be so much as a spot of yellow on the leaves, although some of the heads may have those little yellow flowers. The leaves should be dark green and the stalks the deep jade of broccoli. In the fall you can find broccoli di rape loose in the farmers' markets where you will find some delicate, tender stalks and some thick with tightly curled flower heads that make its resemblance to broccoli very clear.

What you are after is the flower heads, although a few leaves look very pretty and taste good, too. The thicker the stalk the more it may require trimming. The secret is not to undercook. Undercooked broccoli di rape is tough and rubbery. Slightly overcooked it is tender and silky. It is hard to make a confession like this in these health-obsessed times, but I like vegetables to be *very* tender. I like a string bean that *gives* and does not fight back. I am also very fond of the sort of stewed vegetables you get in Middle Eastern restaurants: string beans and okra that have been cooked in a sauce for hours.

Broccoli di rape stews up nicely, too, in broth, butter and garlic. You can add it to a soup, or serve it cold with avocado and a ginger dressing as a first course. It would make an admirable addition to a bacon and spinach salad. With buckwheat noodles it makes a filling and very nutritious lunch, and of course you can serve it as a side vegetable. But its most magnificent incarnation is in a three-part dish called Pepper Chicken with Polenta and Broccoli di Rape, which is perfect for supper in late fall.

PEPPER CHICKEN WITH POLENTA AND BROCCOLI DI RAPE

serves 4

1 chicken (fryer)
1 tablespoon dried thyme
½ tablespoon black pepper
1 teaspoon red pepper flakes
2 teaspoons brown sugar
1 dash ground clove
paprika
3 cloves garlic, slivered
butter
1-1 ½ pounds broccoli di rape

THE CHICKEN

1. Have the butcher cut up your chicken (or do it yourself), separating leg from thigh and splitting the breast into quarters. The idea is to have pieces of uniform size.

2. Make a dry marinade by combining thyme, black pepper, red pepper flakes, brown sugar and ground clove. Sprinkle this on both sides of the chicken and set aside for an hour or so. When it is time to put the chicken in the oven, dust it with paprika, festoon with slivered garlic and dot with butter.

3. Bake as you ordinarily bake chicken. There is no rule for this. Some people like their chicken falling off the bone (I am one of these) and some feel that this is an abomination and prefer theirs just done. Whichever way you prefer, make sure the chicken becomes crisp.

THE POLENTA

4. Make the polenta in the ordinary way. I have found it useful to stir it with a whisk. Add a nice piece of butter while you are stirring: boil 6½ cups water and add cornmeal slowly when the water begins to simmer. Keep stirring for about twenty minutes. The polenta is done when it pulls away from the pot.

THE BROCCOLI DI RAPE

5. While you are stirring, steam one large bunch (about a pound to a pound and a half) of broccoli di rape from which you have removed any woody stalks and unnecessary leaves.

ASSEMBLING THE DISH

6. Turn the polenta onto a large platter. Arrange the chicken pieces all around and then pour on top of the polenta all the pan juices, which includes all the chicken fat and butter. Remember, this is a party dish and not something you are going to

serve every day. If there is not enough pan juice, add olive oil,
butter or both and a little lemon juice.
7. Put the broccoli di rape on top of the polenta, or arrange it in
some graceful way on the side of the platter. I like mine on top.
Then dig in.

This is an amazingly delectable dish and serves to show off
bitter greens at their best: they bring out the taste of everything
else while contributing their own pungent contrast.

Furthermore, this dish is popular with men, but do not expect
them to finish the meal with an endive salad.

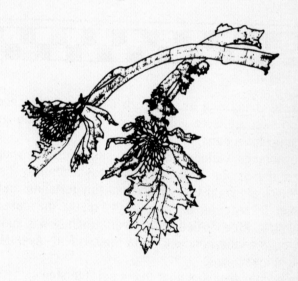

SOUP

There is nothing like soup. It is by its nature eccentric: no two are ever alike, unless of course you get your soup from cans.

Soup embraces variety. There are silken cream soups that glisten on the spoon and spicy bisques with tiny flecks of lobster. There are broths in which float tiny tortellini and bouillons served in teacups on cold days, or, in the case of my great-aunt Julia Rice, ladled from silver punch bowls and served in punch cups to the conductors on the old Fifth Avenue streetcar during snowstorms.

There are cold soups, soups that resemble stews, but when I think about soup, I mean something you eat with bread and butter and call a meal—meat soups and bean soups: thick, warming and consoling, and also a good way to deal with leftovers.

The best soup I have ever eaten was made from a friend's leftover Christmas pheasant, the remains of the potatoes Anna, peas, cabbage and stock. Not so long ago I bought a pheasant at my local farmers' market and served it roasted to my family only so that I could try to replicate it. But that soup, like most leftover soups, is a kind of lost chord and no one will ever find it again.

Soup is the food of childhood, and I remember being brought up on Campbell's vegetarian vegetable soup, which contained, and still may contain, okra and lentils among the traditional corn, peas and string beans.

When we were ailing my mother made what she called chicken soup but is really poached chicken made with chicken breasts, carrots, onions, a strip of lemon peel, some peppercorns and spring water. After two hours of the gentlest poaching, it is done. You serve it in a soup plate with toast points and flat ginger ale to invalids of every kind.

It was not until I was a teenager that I tasted lentil soup which became a lifetime companion. There have been periods of my life when I have lived on lentil soup—made with veal bones, without bones, with spinach, tomatoes, potatoes, leftover baked chicken or steak. After having composed about ten thousand lentil soups, all of them good (since lentil soup is never bad), I have found that the most successful of all lentil soups calls for veal bones and leftover veal stew.

I could eat soup every day of the week, and now that I have a small child I have come to believe that it is curative. Chicken soup really does seem to help a cold, and there is nothing for intestinal disturbances like barley soup.

There is almost no soup I find alien, although I do not like the idea of sweet fruit soup. I have made summer soups in the blender of yogurt and cucumber, and I would like to make fish soup but I am married to a man who feels that fish must only be grilled. In a perfect world I would have a real freezer in which I would keep ice cube trays of frozen stock, or I would do what cooking magazines encourage: freeze the stock in ice trays, crack the cubes into bags and label neatly. I would also have little jars of meat glaze, stock that has been reduced until it resembles what Father Robert Farrar Capon calls "a tender shoe heel" and makes the ultimate soup base if you can stop yourself from eating it straight out of the jar.

But we do not live in a perfect world, which is too bad since canned broth is pretty nasty. All soups are better for having been made of fresh stock, but some soups do all right with plain water.

There must be more recipes for soup than any other thing. It is a true convenience food and has been since Esau sold his birthright for a plate of lentil soup. Vegetables simmered in plain water with herbs and a little butter make a fine soup and so do beans and meat, which must be simmered for hours. Even these soups are easy: you put them on the stove and leave them alone.

There is one soup I make all winter long which has the double virtue of being scrumptious and effortless. It is full of good things. You make it in the morning and eat it in the evening. All you have to do is skim the fat off the top. The second day you can add to it to change it, if you have any left over.

The meat for this soup is short ribs. There is nothing like it for soup, but it is fatty: shin makes a good enough substitute. Trim as much fat as you can from the short ribs, which can be kept in one piece or cut up by the butcher.

BEEF, LEEK
AND BARLEY SOUP

serves 3-4

2 big, meaty short ribs
½ cup barley
3 large cloves garlic, chopped
2 onions, chopped
3 large leeks, cut lengthwise
black pepper
8 cups filtered water or beef stock
other vegetables (optional)

1. Trim short ribs and put them on the bottom of your soup pot.
2. Add barley, garlic, onions, and leeks (use both the white and the green parts). You can also add mushrooms and any other vegetables you might like. Grind in a little black pepper.
3. Add filtered water or beef stock and let simmer on the back burner for at least three hours while you go about your business.
(You can add lima beans, cubed potatoes, peas, corn, string beans and chopped tomatoes. I myself would not put any kind of squash into this soup, and I am not fond of turnips.)
4. Before serving, skim off the fat, take the meat off the bones, chop it and put it back in the soup.

This sort of soup makes a meal, and if you are not feeding intimidating company, you can serve it *as* the meal. A little dish of pasta, followed by soup, bread and cheese and a salad makes a very heartwarming dinner, with grapes and chocolate cookies for dessert.

Soup has come to symbolize the ultimate in comfort and safety. Many years ago, when I was about fifteen, I saw someone served a cup of soup, and this vision, which had all the sentimental charm of a painting by Sir Edwin Landseer, is indelibly imprinted on my mind.

It was a cold, rainy autumn night and some grubby teenagers had gathered at a friend's rather splendid house. We heard the crunch of a car on gravel. A taxi pulled up and into the wet night stepped the friend's older sister, who was coming home from college for the weekend. She was probably nineteen but she looked like the picture of sophistication. She wore brown pumps, a green tweed suit, pearl earrings and her hair was pulled back in a French twist.

She took off her wet coat, sat down in front of the fire and her mother brought her a large, ornamental bone china cup of soup. She warmed her hands on the cup and then she set it on its saucer, balanced it on her lap and ate the soup with a bouillon spoon. The dog, a weimaraner, lay dozing at her feet. Outside the rain clattered. Inside that pretty living room all was safe.

Of course you need not have a weimaraner or a fire or anyone coming home from college. To feel safe and warm on a cold wet night, all you really need is soup.

ENGLISH FOOD

If you work up the courage to confess that you like English food people are apt to sneer and tell you that it is impossible to get a decent meal in the British Isles and that the English know nothing about cooking. Even the English, some of whom have been brought up on a dread substance known as School Food, often feel this way.

England, of course, has a long and grand tradition of cooking—it is a much plainer and more forthright variety than that of France and, since it is of a cold climate, it does not have the sun-drenched style of, say, Italian food, but it has pleasures all its own.

The first time I went to England I was a student and virtually penniless. I can't remember what I ate except a plate of custard at a café near Victoria Station and a gooseberry bread pudding in Canterbury. A slightly richer friend took me out for tea one afternoon at a place called Heals in the Tottenham Court Road.

Heals in the early sixties was a cross between Hammacher-Schlemmer, Design Research and the present-day Conran's. It sold top-of-the-line pots and pans and fixtures. Young marrieds furnished their households at Heals, where you could get linens, lamps, knives, forks, plates and so on. On the top was a tea-room, which has since vanished.

We sat down to tea and I was in heaven. This was the wish fulfillment of a childhood filled with English children's books. It seemed a wonderful feast to me as a child and now that I am grown up tea is my favorite meal. But until I sat down at Heals I had never had a proper tea in my life.

All around us were real Englishwomen—there did not seem to be a man in the place—pouring out tea from brown teapots. Put before us was a plate of bread and butter, a seed cake and a dish of little cakes made with candied cherries. I felt I would never be as happy again as I was that afternoon.

On my next trip I stayed with my friend Richard Davies and his parents. At the Davieses' I was introduced to the institution of English Sunday lunch: roast meat, potatoes, two vegetables and a sweet. I learned that even when the papers bore the banner headline: WHEW! WHAT A SCORCHER! the meal never varied. You might sit around the swimming pool at someone's country house and still emerge to be fed roast leg of lamb, roast pota-toes, two vegetables and dessert.

It was on this second trip that I had my first cream tea, which many people feel is in itself the perfect meal: scones, clotted cream and strawberry jam. As you drive out of London you begin to see signs on houses that read WE DO CREAM TEAS. My cream tea was consumed at a tea house in Woodstock, right near Blenheim Palace, on a day thick with clouds. The tea shop had one large room full of tables dressed in white cloths. We sat down and consumed an amazing quantity of scones, cream and jam.

On my next trip I was more grown up, better heeled, and I decided it would be nice to do some cooking. I found myself wandering happily in the local shops and supermarkets where everything was so pleasingly different from what I saw at home. A trip to the Harrods food hall filled me with awe. I have never seen anything to compare with it: the dozens of local cheeses and the variety of imported ones. The numbers of birds and kinds of eggs. The fish, pâtés, and cuts of meat I had never heard of.

In England you could get chicken that tasted like chicken, and gooseberries and tomatoes and those long pale green cucumbers with a silvery taste. In specialty shops there were raised pies: veal, ham and egg, chicken, and cottage pie. You could buy a bag of delicious cream cakes and eat them in the movies. You could even find a decent cup of coffee, although nothing compares to plain old English tea.

To divert me from my endless meanderings in food stores, Richard took me on a trip to the Highlands of Scotland, where we were assured we would never find anything edible at all. On a freezing night in June we had dinner in our hotel and we decided to order haggis, as a joke. Haggis is the national dish of Scotland. It is composed of minced liver and oatmeal (barley is a variation) in a savory sauce, stuck into a sheep's stomach and boiled. It is served with something called "mashed neeps," which are turnips. It sounded so dire that we felt we ought to try it.

The haggis was brought to our table in its stomach bag which was slashed before our eyes. Out slid the contents, which gave off a very delicious smell. To our amazement, we loved it. It was rich, savory, just right for a cold place and perfect with the slightly bitter turnips.

While wandering around the Highlands we ate magnificent smoked salmon, soused herring, wonderful bread and biscuits and something called Scotch tablet, which is a solidified bar of butter and sugar.

It is possible to get nasty food everywhere, but with the exception of a few eccentric meals fed me by my peers, the only awful thing I ever ate in England was a packaged pork pie; but then a person who eats a packaged pork pie gets what she deserves.

Once the English food addict is back on home turf it is

possible to stave off pangs of longing with the aid of any number of English cookbooks from which you can make such wonderful things as Queen of Puddings, Easter biscuits, potted shrimp, ginger cake, lemon sponge, Bath buns, orange custard, Lancashire hot pot and crumpets, which I have attempted many times, never with any success.

My copies of Jane Grigson's *English Food* and Mrs. Florence White's *Good Things in England* are falling apart. For late night reading I enjoy Mrs. Arthur Webb's *Farmhouse Cookery*, which has no copyright date but looks to have been published in the twenties and has descriptions of the Welsh Grate, the Devon Down Oven, the Suffolk frying pan and contains recipes for things like Whitby Polony (a kind of sandwich filling of minced beef, ham and bread crumbs) and Singing Hinnies (a griddle cake). I am also fond of Alison Utely's *Recipes from an Old Farm House*, which describes a pudding made from the milk of a newly calved cow should you happen to have one around the house.

One of my greatest finds, in an old bookshop in the Hamptons, is a copy of *From Caviar to Candy: Recipes for Small Households from All Parts of the World*, by Mrs. Phillip Martineau. First published in 1927, it covers the territory from hors d'oeuvres to sweets and poses such questions as: "Now, why, I ask, should the same old fare be invariably provided at cricket lunches? I remember a cricket lunch at Hurlingham Club in the Argentine . . ." Her first chapter, entitled "Cooks—Mistresses and Imaginations," sets the tone: "What chance has the average cook, unless her mistress will help her?" she asks. This is a question I have asked myself many times.

Her recipes are more chatty than scientific—"There be some that claim that it is worthwhile even to visit that dullest of all dull places, Bagnolle de l'Orne, to eat the tripe prepared at a nearby town" begins one.

When it comes to cakes and puddings, savories, bread and tea cakes, the English cannot be surpassed. If you love English food there are many things you can make at home and you can find things at specialty stores. But the one thing you can never find, which lovers of English food dream about at night, is double cream.

When the English come to the United States and see what we call cream they cannot believe their eyes. What we call heavy cream they get for free on the top of their unhomogenized milk, which is delivered in glass bottles by actual milkmen.

When Americans see what the English call cream, they cannot believe *their* eyes.

My first encounter with double cream took place at my first encounter with English Sunday lunch at the Davieses' house in the country. We had just finished our roast beef and it was time for dessert. Out came a bowl of raspberries and a large gravy boat.

"What's in there?" I said.

"Cream," they said.

I turned the gravy boat slantwise but nothing poured out. I felt this might be some sort of joke since all eyes were on me. I gave the gravy boat a little shake but nothing emerged.

"Try a spoon," said Richard's mother.

I did, and what I scooped out was the consistency of cold molasses or very thick, homemade mayonnaise. I plopped it onto my berries.

"This is *cream*?" I gasped.

"Double cream," they said.

Since it was the most delicious thing I had ever eaten, I went on a kind of binge of double cream, which, it seemed miraculous to me, you could simply go into a grocery store and buy. I especially liked it slathered on little pancakes that came six to a package. McVittie's Scotch Pancakes have now disappeared off the face of the earth.

Back in the States, so great was my longing for double cream that when Richard, who lived in New York, went home for Christmas, I asked him if he would bring me a pint.

I met him at the airport one cold January night. He emerged from Customs, tall and rattled-looking, carrying a dripping bag out in front of him as if it were a wet fish. His coat sleeve and his shoes were covered in double cream. The lid had slipped off in the bag, the container had slipped sideways and the resulting mess caused considerable interest among the Customs inspectors.

"What is that?" said the Customs man to Richard.

"It's cream, for a friend," Richard said. The Customs man gave him a hard look, and then his face softened. He spoke gently, as if to an insane person.

"We have dairy products in the United States, too, Mr. Davies," he said.

But anyone who has been to England could have told him that we don't have cream.

WITHOUT SALT

As a child, while my sister busied herself mooshing the chocolate candies to see which had the best centers, I was happily licking the salt off the pretzels and leaving their sticky bodies on the rug. To show off my manual dexterity, I liked to take the pimientos out of the stuffed olives and stick the olives on my fingers. In this way, I could easily polish off an entire little jar, and my craving for pickled onions was considered advanced in one so young.

All my favorite foods were salty. I would gladly forgo ice cream for potato chips. I adored bacon, pickles and peanuts. As I grew up and became more sophisticated I graduated to prosciutto, anchovies, sun-dried tomatoes, Genoa salami, tapenade and Niçoise olives. If nothing salty was around, I simply ate salt. As a college student I was asked by my geology instructor why I had failed to identify my halite crystal. The reason was that I had *eaten* my halite crystal.

I was also in the habit of salting my bread, even though I used only sweet butter. How happy I was when someone gave me a salt grinder for a present! How lovely those crunchy little grains tasted on top of Italian butter and semolina bread, and in a pinch, I simply took off the top of the grinder and ate the grains right out of the jar.

So I was brought low, to say the least, when I was informed by my doctor that if I did not quit my evil ways I would end up with hypertension.

I wended my way home from the doctor's office unhappily thinking of all the things I would have to do without. From the bus window I could see throngs of people eating pizza and soft pretzels, many of them looking a good deal less healthy than I. That night as I sat in my kitchen hoping that my tears might improve the awfulness of my salt-free cottage cheese, I felt sorrier for myself than I had ever felt. Nothing, I was sure, would ever taste good anymore. What was life without goat cheese? Virginia ham? Lime pickle?

I brushed my tears away and decided to meet my fate squarely and with a courageous heart. I figured that if I had to do without all the salty things I loved, I would simply buy the best of everything that wasn't salty: the finest olive oil, raspberry vinegar, fresh unsalted mozzarella cheese, Normandy butter, very fresh garlic, chili peppers and ginger.

Going salt-free often costs more money, I discovered. You can buy salt-free chicken broth in the health food stores and it costs about a dollar more than the kind you can buy in the supermarket. It also takes more time. To make a good salt-free soup, you have to start with extra rich broth which can only be made at home. And some salt-free things, like cottage cheese, are hopeless. Others, like saltless Cheddar cheese, are not half bad and some—saltless potato chips—are actually wonderful.

After a couple of weeks I felt I had gotten the hang of my new regime. I had discovered saltless bread, smoked mozzarella, green peppercorns and fresh sage. I felt I might venture out into the real world for a meal. I did, and I was shocked. How incredibly salty everything was! A bite of ham seemed almost inedible. A Chinese meal brought a buzz to my head and tears to my eyes. I scrambled home to the safety of my now pure kitchen and had myself some tiny new potatoes with a little pepper, a slice of bread with dark green olive oil and some chopped scallions and a sliced kirby cucumber with nothing on it at all.

Without salt, things taste like themselves. Many critics of American agribusiness claim that our national salt addiction is the result of an attempt to get some flavor into our denatured produce. These critics are doubtless right, so the salt-free person must treat himself well. It is possible to eat happily even if your idea of a reasonable sandwich is, as mine used to be, a salt bagel, cream cheese and *Büdnerfleisch*, a salty, air-dried beef from Switzerland.

It is even possible to make a delicious salad dressing without a speck of salt. It is inspiring to make your own vinegar by steeping shallots, or sage leaves or fresh hot chili peppers, basil or rosemary. The salt-free person must make his own condiments since most sauces—mustard, catsup, horseradish or Worcestershire—are loaded with salt. Angostura bitters, however, are salt-free and delicious added to a salad dressing.

I am now a better, slightly thinner person because of this regime. I am a little tired of cooking down the tomatoes to get something that resembles tomato paste (which is very salty), but it is worth it. I have a shelf full of interesting vinegars, and another of delicious oils, and I no longer explain to friends who come for supper that nothing has been salted. I keep in mind that when I feed people without salt, I am actually doing them a favor.

For a salt-free dinner party I suggest:

BAKED CHICKEN
WITH GARLIC AND APPLES

serves 4-6

2 small frying chickens cut up
paprika, pepper
as many unpeeled cloves of garlic as you like
6 McIntosh apples
butter

1. *Sprinkle the chicken with paprika and pepper. It is worthwhile to go to a spice store for the paprika—the fresher the better.*
2. *Do not peel the garlic, but remove any obvious tough outer layer.*
3. *Cut the apples in fourths and core.*
4. *Lay the garlic and apples among the chicken pieces.*
5. *Dot with butter and bake as long as you like chicken to bake.*
6. *The apples will have cooked down, and the garlic cloves can be eaten skin and all.*

Because you have used two chickens for four people, you will have leftovers. Therefore you can treat yourself the next day to

COLD ROAST CHICKEN
WITH BUCKWHEAT NOODLES

1. *Slice the leftover chicken into strips.*
2. *Boil the noodles (available in health food and Oriental stores) according to directions on the package. Drain under cold water.*
3. *Place the chicken over the noodles. Add chopped scallions and dress with the following:*

SALAD DRESSING WITH GINGER

1. *Grate a small knob of ginger—about half an inch.*
2. *Mix the grated ginger into ½ cup of finest olive oil.*
3. *Add 1 to 1½ tablespoons vinegar.*
4. *Steep one smashed garlic clove in the dressing for a few minutes.*

Pour this over the chicken and noodles, and you will never miss salt again.

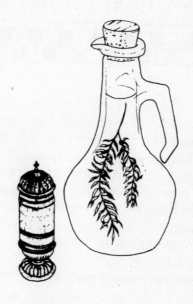

STUFFING: A CONFESSION

It was years before I could come out and say how much I hated stuffing. Everyone in the world but me was fired by an elemental urge to fill up bird cavities with this and that. At Thanksgiving time, friends would proudly confide their stuffing recipes, many of which I found personally nauseating: dried bread, prunes, oysters and water chestnuts, for example. Prunes and oysters! If such a dish were set before you at a restaurant, you would flee in horror and dismay, but when it comes to stuffing, anything goes. People get to make up disgusting combinations and then stuff their poor turkeys with them.

Holiday after holiday I would push my portion around on my plate. After all, you cannot say to those near and dear to you: "I think your stuffing tastes like sawdust flavored with sage and it has the consistency of lumpy library paste." Everyone else loved it. It was clear that I was in opposition to a national tradition.

But I did not realize how emotionally charged an issue stuffing was until I decided to make Thanksgiving dinner on my own for the first time. After years at my parents' and sister's, I felt it was my turn to do things my way.

"What are you going to give us?" my sister wanted to know.

"Baked brussels sprouts. Chestnuts and onions. Green salad. Ginger cake. An unstuffed turkey."

"A *what*?"

"I don't like stuffing," I said. "I never have. This is my big chance not to have any."

"But there's no *point* to turkey without stuffing," she said.

"But that is the point. I love turkey and I do not see it as a mere vehicle for the stuffing. This way, the turkey will be prominent."

"I don't know if I can get the kids to come," she said, referring to my four stuffing-mad nieces.

When Thanksgiving came, everyone liked the turkey, but they all seemed a little downcast. Something was missing—the stuffing.

"An unstuffed turkey is more elegant," I said. But no one seemed to care.

The next year I acquired some in-laws and went to their house for Thanksgiving. My in-laws are Latvian. When they came to this country, turkey presented a challenge to my mother-in-law, who, since she had never seen an American turkey, treated it as a large game bird. She poached turkey thighs until tender, ground them in a meat grinder, mixed them with cooked rice, salt and pepper, and stuffed the bird. Then she pressed peppercorns against the side of the turkey, wrapped it in bacon and roasted it. The result was exceedingly good, and it made me realize that I was the only person in America who had ever thought of going without stuffing. I would have to adjust.

Shortly after that, I tasted the first bread stuffing I actually liked. It calls for butter, cream, sweet Italian sausage, mushrooms, celery, garlic, *fresh* sage and the torn-out insides of two loaves of Italian bread, with a beaten egg added after everything has been amalgamated and the bread has soaked up a quantity of butter and cream.

"This has possibilities," I said.

At night some people count sheep and others read mysteries. I lie in bed and think about food. Often I make up menus. Sometimes I invent recipes. One night, while drowsily meditating on the issue of stuffing, it came to me: cornbread and prosciutto. Yes, that was it! The perfect stuffing. The next Thanksgiving, I tried it out.

"I'm stuffing the turkey this year," I told my sister. She was much relieved.

"What with?" she said.

"Cornbread and prosciutto," I said.

"I wonder what it will taste like," she said. I did not find this an encouraging response.

CORNBREAD AND PROSCIUTTO STUFFING

for a 17-20 lb. bird

soup stock (see step 1)
1 stick butter
2 medium yellow onions, diced
1 leek, diced
1 large clove garlic, minced
½ pound prosciutto, diced
1 pound cornmeal stuffing (see step 4)
black pepper to taste
1 scallion, chopped
1 head Italian parsley, chopped

1. Make a rich stock out of the giblets, wing tips and neck (if you can stand not to roast it) of the turkey, along with some chicken parts and an onion. Let simmer for several hours. Makes about two cups.

2. Melt butter in a large saucepan and add onions, leek (white and tender green part) and garlic. Wilt these in the butter.

3. Add prosciutto (for people who do not eat pork products, dried funghi porcini and toasted pecans make an admirable substitute) and sauté briefly.

4. Slowly add the contents of two bags of cornmeal stuffing if you are lazy or the equivalent amount (about sixteen ounces) of fresh cornmeal stuffing if you are not, fresh ground black pepper to taste, scallion and parsley, and sauté until the bread is coated with the butter.

5. Moisten with broth until fluffy but not wet. This is enough for a seventeen-pound turkey with some left over to cook in a pot as a side dish.

Before tasting it, I wondered if it was wise to cook from recipes that come to you when you are in a semiconscious state, but this stuffing was universally loved. It made everyone happy, and it made them feel that everything was right again. After all, an unstuffed turkey is like a jigsaw puzzle of the American flag with a piece missing right in the middle. Now I had been brought to my senses and all was restored to order.

The next year I caught my sister stealing spoonsful of it from the casserole, and if I hadn't stopped her, she would have stuck her fork right into the turkey cavity.

No one ever says: "Cornbread and prosciutto. I wonder what it will taste like."

Instead, they say the words every cook longs to hear: "This is wonderful. May I please have some more?"

FLANK STEAK: THE NEGLECTED CUT

Standing ribs are the king of beef, and filet mignon is the prince. The flank steak is a humble serf, lean, workmanlike and with no pretense to anything grand. It is seen as an inferior cut—the sort of thing you have for family dinner but not for a dinner party.

My introduction to flank steak was a dreary one. I was invited for supper by a colleague who told me she was no cook, but that flank steak, according to the recipe of her sainted grandmother, was her one dish. Because I like to hang around in the kitchens of others, I watched while my colleague took a flat, blade-shaped piece of meat which she then rolled up and tied, like an old carpet. This was plopped into a kettle of hot water and set to boil for what seemed an awfully long time. While it cooked we stuffed ourselves with bread and cheese and then it was time to eat.

I was told that this was an old-fashioned dish and it may have been. It had the texture of poached rope and I have never had the nerve to try it again.

Boiled beef is a noble thing. The soul—even the soul of a

person who eats red meat five times a year—cries out for it every once in a while. It is *mean* to boil a flank steak when there are so many other cuts—shin, rump, bottom round—crying out to be boiled. A flank steak should be grilled over a wood fire or broiled in the broiler, or not cooked at all.

If people are not boiling their flank steaks, they are often stuffing them, and why not? Because flank steak is flat it looks as if it would take well to stuffing. Some people pat on the stuffing, roll, tie and then pot roast their steak. Others cut a pocket in the poor little steak and then cook it to death. This is wrong, all wrong. No one would dream of boiling a rib roast or stuffing a filet. But because flank steak looks as if it can take whatever punishment is dished out, people feel drawn to misuse it.

The result of these methods is gray and stringy. When Cubans overcook a flank steak at least they call it *ropa viejo*—"old clothes." To cook a flank steak properly, you must first contemplate its many virtues.

First of all, it is very tender when sliced on the diagonal. It has a wonderful beefy taste and is also nice and juicy. Because it is thinner at the ends than in the center, people who crave rare and those who demand well done can both be made happy.

Furthermore, it is cheap, and it is good hot, lukewarm or cold. It takes brilliantly to marinating and if you are lucky enough to have any left over it can be minced and put in a lentil salad, or eaten cold on toast for breakfast.

Because it must be grilled *fast* it can be made at the last minute, and is thus perfect for unexpected guests or when you feel you must have a good dinner but don't want to cook ahead. It is properly sliced paper thin and a little goes a long way. It also looks lovely on a platter.

Although I am not much of a beef eater, I am loyal to the flank steak. It is delicious in any season of the year. In the summer it can be broiled in the morning and sliced cold in the evening. Furthermore, it has very little fat. Considering these many splendors, who would want to boil it?

No matter what you do to it, the method of cooking is always the same. You lay the steak flat in a pan and put it under the broiler or over the coals for about five minutes (or less for rare) per side. It is not a terrible thing to slice into it to see how it is doing, but it is not a good idea to do this more than once.

After it is cooked, let it sit for five minutes or so and then slice it on the diagonal into thin slices and arrange it on a platter. The juice from the meat makes an excellent sauce.

The plainest way to cook it involves painting your steak with olive oil, rubbing it with garlic and seasoning it with fresh black pepper.

The simplest marinade consists of olive oil, garlic, soy sauce and lemon juice. To make something that resembles steak teri-yaki, add a teaspoon or so of honey.

My particular favorite is curried flank steak, for which you must make your own curry: the powdered kind simply will not do. You can balance the following ingredients to suit yourself: turmeric, paprika, ginger, cumin, dry mustard, a little ground clove and cinnamon. Add olive oil, a drop of soy sauce and mix to a thick sludge. Anoint the flank steak with this delicious paste, stud with garlic and let it sit. You can either marinate this all day long, or for an hour before cooking.

When you have grilled and sliced it, add the meat juices to the cooking pan and pour over the meat.

I also like to use a dry, very peppery marinade of crushed red pepper, black pepper, thyme, a pinch of ground clove and a half teaspoon of dark brown sugar. Rub this on the meat, stud with garlic and let it sit. Naturally, the garlic is removed before grilling.

Now let us pretend you served flank steak for a dinner party of four people and there are a few slices left over. If you come from the sort of family that finds steak on toast for breakfast disgust-ing (I come from a family that finds cold steak on toast delight-ful), you will be able to have cold beef and lentil salad for dinner. Shred, slice or dice the flank steak and dress it with olive oil, pepper, whatever pan juices were left over and some wine vinegar. Cook a cup of lentils in the usual way, drain, cool and dress with olive oil, garlic, scallions, pepper (or some minced, fresh hot pepper) and vinegar. Combine the lentils and the beef and serve with watercress.

In my house, however, any leftover flank steak is gone by lunchtime. I am fortunate that I am married to a man who finds leftovers for breakfast repellent: I don't have anyone to fight. As children, my sister and I fought bitterly over any cold meat that happened to be lying around. A cold steak sandwich *is* sort of disgusting, but it is also sort of wonderful:

1. Toast two slices of whole-wheat bread.

2. Let the bread cool and then generously spread with sweet butter (this is a recipe for people whose cholesterol is too low).

3. Tenderly lay on one layer of sliced flank steak, making sure to include the juices.

4. Add salt and pepper to taste, and enjoy it with a large cup of coffee.

KITCHEN HORRORS

Awful things happen in the kitchen all the time, even to the most experienced cooks, but when they happen to you it is not comforting to know that you are supposed to learn from your mistakes, especially when you contemplate the lurid-looking mess in front of you.

I myself have never made a spinach pie, and therefore I have never had the thrilling opportunity to see one catch on fire. Therefore I have never watched my husband place his large, wet hiking boot on top of my flaming puff pastry to keep it from burning down the house, but this did happen to a friend. More mundane things happen to me: half the cake sticks in the bundt pan. The pudding won't unmold from the pudding mold, and when it does, half of it is melted.

A really first-rate disaster passes into legend. My sister and I have never forgotten the salmon loaf our mother, an excellent cook, made when we were little. By mistake, she reached for the cayenne pepper instead of the paprika. I was six, my sister was ten and we remember it as if it were yesterday.

My husband recalls a dinner party he attempted to give as a

young man around town. The beef stew turned into an ocean of gray juice in which tiny, hard cubes of overcooked meat floated. The dessert was to be crêpes but when he removed the batter from the refrigerator, something had gone terribly amiss. The batter had turned into cinder block, and the wooden spoon he had left in it was stuck. Later it turned out that he had used potato starch instead of flour. These things happen.

My own greatest disasters have been the result of inexperience, overreaching, intimidation and self-absorption.

As a blithe young thing I became quite hipped on a dish called rösti—a Swiss way of frying shredded potatoes in an enormous quantity of butter. I had been introduced to this dish by an English boyfriend, who loved to entertain. One night he invited six people for dinner and I thought it would be a swell idea to make rösti.

Alone in my beloved's kitchen, I began to shred the potatoes into a big bowl. By the time my arm began to get sore, I noticed that the potatoes had taken on a pinkish tinge, but I pressed on. A few minutes later, I looked to see how many more potatoes I needed and observed that a sickly green was now the predominant shade. A few minutes later, my heartthrob appeared.

"Good gracious," he said. "What's this funny black stuff?"

There was no doubt about it. That funny black stuff was my potatoes. Into the garbage they went, and to this day I am still a little phobic about potatoes: rösti for two, potato pancakes for four is my motto.

In the middle period of my kitchen disasters, by which time I had done a lot of cooking and knew my way around the kitchen, I decided to entrap the man I would later marry by baking a red snapper, the only fish he liked. Misguided by passion, I decided I would stuff this fish with sliced grapes, small shrimp and fermented black beans. I had never stuffed a fish before, let alone baked one. I had no idea what I was doing. In fact, I must have been out of my mind. I had no recipe to guide me, but does love need a recipe? Does inspiration require instructions?

It is hard to describe the result, which was put back into the oven many times before it dried out and became inedible. Many were my maidenly blushes as I said: "Well, the inside still looks a little underdone, but I'll just pop it back in the oven for a minute." I might have said this fifteen times.

When it finally emerged from the oven, this fish looked like Hieronymus Bosch's vision of hell, with little nasty-looking things spilling out into a pallid-looking puddle of undercooked fish juices.

Years later, I entertained a newly married friend. This friend had married a goddess and lived in the country. I of course was a slob and lived in the city. The goddess had built their post-and-beam house with her own two hands, raised chickens, milked cows and was a veterinarian as well. On the side she was a glassblower. She had built her own studio. All the glassware, jugs, pitchers and vases in their house were made by her. Of course she baked her own bread, raised her own vegetables and made her own clothes, although she didn't yet know how to spin. At that news I heaved a sigh of relief.

As the burden of this woman's accomplishments was being piled ever higher on my lowly shoulders, I cooked dinner. Baked chicken, hominy in cream, steamed string beans. By the time I heard about the glassblowing, I was whipping up some butterscotch brownies for dessert.

It was the first meal I have ever cooked of which there was not enough. I don't mean that my husband and our friend polished everything off because it was so delicious. They polished everything off because there was so little to polish, and there were no seconds. My butterscotch brownies would compensate, I thought. They were cooling in their pan on a rack, and when I went to cut them, I knew that something awful had happened.

I did not think that substituting Demerara sugar for white sugar would make much of a difference, but the knife wouldn't seem to penetrate. When I finally sawed through to the bottom, I realized that the sugar had settled to the bottom and solidified. Oh, well, I thought. It will be like Scotch tablet, that delicious confection of butter and sugar.

But those butterscotch brownies were not like Scotch tablet. They were like cooked sugar that had turned into firebrick. From this experience I learned that you should never be in the kitchen with anyone married to a perfect person.

My greatest horror, however, was a culinary triumph, in my opinion. *In my opinion* are the crucial words.

I had been invited to the country for Easter. At the same time an English friend had sent me a packet of suet. With this I intended to make something called Suffolk Pond Pudding from Jane Grigson's wonderful book *English Food.*

Suffolk Pond Pudding, although something of a curiosity, sounded perfectly splendid. First, you line a pudding basin with suet crust. Then you cut butter mixed with sugar into small pieces. Next you take an entire lemon and prick it all over with a fork. Then you stick the lemon on top of the butter and sugar, surround it with more butter and sugar, stick a pastry lid on the top, tie it up in a pudding cloth and steam in a kettle for four hours. It never occurred to me that nobody might want to eat it.

I followed every step carefully. My suet crust was masterful. When unwrapped from its cloth, the crust was a beautiful, deep honey color. I turned it out onto an ornamental plate.

My hostess looked confused. "It looks like a baked hat," she said.

"It looks like the Alien," said my future husband.

"Never mind," I said. "It will be the most delicious thing you ever tasted."

The pudding was brought to the table. My host and hostess, my future husband and a woman guest looked at it suspiciously. I cut the pudding. As Jane Grigson had promised, out ran a lemon-scented buttery toffee. I sliced up the lemon, which was soft and buttery too. Each person was to get some crust, a slice of lemon and some sauce.

What a hit! I thought. Exactly the sort of thing I adored. I looked around me happily, and my happiness turned to ash.

My host said: "This tastes like lemon-flavored bacon fat."

"I'm sure it's wonderful," said my hostess. "I mean, in England."

The woman guest said: "This is awful."

My future husband remained silent, not a good sign. I had promised him a swell dessert and here was this weird, inedible sludge from outer space. The others ate ice cream. I ate almost the entire pudding myself.

I have had a number of small horrors since then, mostly involving pie crust, something I haven't quite gotten the hang of. One of my pies fell apart. One was so odd-looking my husband took a picture of it, and one had the texture and resilience of old parchment.

Now that I am more accomplished I feel that I am in a position to gauge my kitchen disasters and choose them carefully. For my next I am either going to make Circassian chicken (poached chicken blanketed with a walnut purée) or a chocolate jelly roll which my sister assures me is a snap to make. I have never cooked either of these things before, but instinct tells me that the possibilities for something going terribly wrong in either case are endless.

ABOUT SALAD

A salad is an abused, neglected thing. Everyone laughs when the waiter in *Ninotchka* says to Greta Garbo, who has ordered a plate of chopped greens: "Madame, this is a restaurant, not a meadow."

In some restaurants these days, the meadow is thrown in without much thought, or given away free, as if to unload it.

The hapless diner may be confronted by a small, fake wooden bowl containing the chopped carcasses of what were once edible plants, usually the unfairly treated romaine, with some depressed red cabbage that has turned blue, dribbled with lurid orange-colored dressing and polka-dotted by a woolly or woody radish. Often a dispirited cherry tomato sits aloft.

Or else a plate appears bearing what resembles a bleached wedge. It *is* a wedge, of almost frozen iceberg lettuce. Or one may meander over to a salad bar and festoon a pile of wilted greens with fake bacon bits, marinated mushrooms, tuna fish, olives, pickled beets, chopped egg, chick peas, canned artichoke hearts and red peppers. This pile is then held together with a kind of thinned library paste studded with crumbs of blue cheese.

No matter how elaborate or simple, the salad is a source of controversy. When to eat it? In the East, after the main course. In the West, before.

Some people feel strongly that salad should be dressed, tossed and served, while others put the dressing in a sauce boat and let each person dress his own.

As for dressing, purists hold that oil, vinegar, salt and pepper—the classic dressing—should never be tampered with in any way. More laid-back types might add dill, or Parmesan cheese, or hot sauce, angostura bitters, lemon juice or mustard. And there are even those who cling to the belief that all dressing must contain a teaspoon of sugar. Others shriek at the very idea.

True extremists, in retaliation against the tendency to drown a salad in dressing, bring to the table a large platter of naked watercress.

Then there are composed salads about which entire books have been written and are believed by some not to be salads at all. They contain meat and fish and cheese. These salads are *complicated.*

The basic point of a salad, as every schoolchild ought to know, is that it is green, quick and easy to fix.

For example, it is lunchtime and you are starving. You are about to make the one bunch of arugula, that most sophisticated of salad greens, into a little salad lunch for yourself when the telephone rings. A starving pal and her baby are going to drop by to visit you and your baby and one bunch of arugula will not feed two. Because invention is the necessity of mothers, you may remember the dish of cold brussels sprouts in the fridge and the jar of walnuts in the pantry. Tossed with a good dressing, these three elements produce a very tasty salad.

Extreme hunger recently propelled me toward this last-minute composition: cold steamed broccoli di rape, avocado, lentil sprouts and watercress. Lentil sprouts, available in health food stores, are crispy and nutlike, while avocado is buttery and smooth. Broccoli di rape is pungent and slightly bitter and watercress has a peppery snap. Together these elements behave rather like the instruments in a string quartet. With the addition of some hard-boiled egg or a little sliced potato, this salad is a meal.

The combinations are endless, especially in summer. In winter, when good lettuce is hard to find, the salad lover can always turn to cold cooked greens: collard with ginger dressing, kale with mustard and garlic, escarole with oil and pepper. Many people eat salad dutifully because they feel it is good for them, but more enlightened types eat it happily because it is good.

If you are sick of tossed salad, get it to lie down and serve it flat. The flat salad makes a good appetizer or first course. This is a salad that is beautifully *placed.* It is not necessary to have gone to Japanese flower arranging classes—all you need is a sharp knife and a nice plate. Paper-thin slices of cucumber, drizzled with garlic dressing and sprinkled with chopped dill, is about as simple a salad as you can get. The slices can be arranged in a circle and wreathed with watercress or those Japanese radish sprouts that are hot enough to bring tears to your eyes.

In the summer, the platter of tomatoes, sliced mozzarella and onion is actually a flat salad and so is a plate of potato, cucumber and tomato with vinaigrette.

These salads *are* good for you—low in calories, high in fiber and vitamins—besides being easy and cheap. But what about a salad that is expensive, complicated to fix and *bad* for you? This salad exists and it is served in the kind of very expensive, old-fashioned restaurant that makes you feel secure and safe while you are there. It is called Salade Gourmande and after you have finished it, instead of feeling light and springy, you feel liverish and heavy, as if your pockets were stuffed with large sums of money.

It is composed of the tenderest inner leaves of Bibb lettuce, tiny cubes of pâté de foie gras and lobster meat. The dressing is primarily French olive oil and the merest drop of vinegar. Here is a salad loaded with cholesterol and fat. It is high on the food chain. It makes you feel guilty for spending a small fortune on a salad.

One New Year's Eve I attempted to feed it to friends. Cutting pâté de foie gras into tiny cubes is a job that makes you gnash your teeth. Buying the cooked lobster meat (a whole lobster is a waste) makes your side hurt as you pay for it. And it takes a lot of Bibb lettuces to provide enough tiny inner leaves.

But never mind—it is worth the half a month's rent it costs.

REPULSIVE DINNERS: A MEMOIR

There is something triumphant about a really disgusting meal. It lingers in the memory with a lurid glow, just as something exalted is remembered with a kind of mellow brilliance. I am not thinking of kitchen disasters—chewy pasta, burnt brownies, curdled sauces: these can happen to anyone. I am thinking about meals that are positively loathsome from soup to nuts, although one is not usually fortunate enough to get either soup or nuts.

Bad food abounds in restaurants, but somehow a bad meal in a restaurant and a bad home-cooked meal are not the same: after all, the restaurant did not invite you to dinner.

My mother believes that people who can't cook should rely on filet mignon and boiled potatoes with parsley, and that they should be on excellent terms with an expensive bakery. But if everyone did that, there would be fewer horrible meals and the rich, complicated tapestry that is the human experience would be the poorer for it.

My life has been much enriched by ghastly meals, two of the awfullest of which took place in London. I am a great champion of English food, but what I was given at these dinners was neither English nor food so far as I could tell.

Once upon a time my old friend Richard Davies took me to a dinner party in Shepherd's Bush, a seedy part of town, at the flat of one of his oldest friends.

"What is he like?" I asked.

"He's a genius," Richard said. "He has vast powers of abstract thought." I did not think this was a good sign.

"How nice," I said. "Can he cook?"

"I don't know," Richard said. "In all these years, I've never had a meal at his house. He's a Scot, and they're very mean."

When the English say "mean," they mean "cheap."

Our host met us at the door. He was a glum, geniusy-looking person and he led us into a large, bare room with a table set for six. There were no smells or sounds of anything being cooked. Two other guests sat in chairs, looking as if they wished there were an hors d'oeuvre. There was none.

"I don't think there will be enough to go around," our host said, as if we were responsible for being so many. Usually, this is not the sort of thing a guest likes to hear but in the end we were grateful that it turned out to be true.

We drank some fairly crummy wine, and then when we were practically gnawing on each other's arms, we were led to the table. The host placed a rather small casserole in the center. We peered at it hopefully. The host lifted the lid. "No peeking," he said.

Usually when you lift the lid of a casserole that has come straight from the oven, some fragrant steam escapes. This did not happen, although it did not immediately occur to me that this casserole had not come straight from the oven, but had been sitting around outside the oven getting lukewarm and possibly breeding salmonella.

Here is what we had: the casserole contained a layer of partially cooked rice, a layer of pineapple rings and a layer of breakfast sausages, all of which was cooked in a liquid of some sort or other. Each person received one pineapple ring, one sausage and a large heap of crunchy rice. We ate in perfect silence, first in shock, then in amazement, and then in gratitude that not only was there not enough to go around, but that nothing else was forthcoming. That was the entire meal.

Later as Richard and I sat in the Pizza Express finishing off a second pie, I said: "Is that some sort of Scottish dish we had tonight?"

"No," said Richard. "It is a genius dish."

Several years later on another trip to London, Richard and I were invited to a dinner party in Hampstead. Our host and hostess lived in a beautiful old house but they had taken out all the old fittings and the place had been redesigned in postindustrial futuristic.

At the door, our hostess spoke these dread words: "I'm trying this recipe out on you. I've never made it before. It's a medieval recipe. It looked very interesting."

Somehow I have never felt that "interesting" is an encouraging word when applied to food.

In the kitchen were two enormous and slightly crooked pies.

"How pretty," I said. "What kind are they?"

"They're medieval fish pies," she said. "A variation on starry gazey pie." Starry gazey pie is one in which the crust is slit so that the whole baked eels within can poke their nasty little heads out and look at the pie crust stars with which the top is supposed to be festooned.

"Oh," I said, swallowing hard. "In what way do they vary?"

"Well, I couldn't get eel," said my hostess. "So I got squid. It has squid, flounder, apples, onions, lots of cinnamon and something called gallingale. It's kind of like frankincense."

"I see," I said.

"It's from the twelfth or thirteenth century," she continued. "The crust is made of flour, water, salt and honey."

I do not like to think very often about that particular meal, but the third was worse.

It took place in suburban Connecticut on a beautiful summer evening. The season had been hot and lush, and the local markets were full of beautiful produce of all kinds. Some friends and I had been invited out to dinner.

"What will we have, do you think?" I asked.

"Our hostess said we weren't having anything special," my friends said. "She said something about an 'old-fashioned fish bake.'"

It is hard to imagine why those four innocent words sounded so ominous in combination.

For hors d'oeuvres we had something which I believe is called cheese food. It is not so much a food as a product. A few tired crackers were lying around with it. Then it was time for dinner.

The old-fashioned fish bake was a terrifying production. Someone in the family had gone fishing and had pulled up a number of smallish fish—no one was sure what kind. These were partially cleaned and not thoroughly scaled and then flung into a roasting pan. Perhaps to muffle their last screams, they were smothered in a thick blanket of sour cream and then pelted with raw chopped onion. As the coup de grâce, they were stuck in a hot oven for a brief period of time until their few juices ran out and the sour cream had a chance to become grainy. With this we were served boiled frozen peas and a salad with iceberg lettuce.

Iceberg lettuce is the cause of much controversy. Many people feel it is an abomination. Others have less intense feelings, but it did seem an odd thing to have when the market five minutes away contained at least five kinds of lettuce, including Oakleaf, Bibb and limestone.

For dessert we had a packaged cheesecake with iridescent cherries embedded in a topping of cerise gum and light tan coffee.

As appears to be traditional with me, a large pizza was the real end of this grisly experience.

But every once in a while, an execrable meal drags on way past the closing times of most pizzerias. You straggle home starving, exhausted, abused in body and spirit. You wonder why you have been given such a miserable dinner, a meal you would not serve to your worst enemy or a junkyard dog. You deserve something delicious to eat, but there is nothing much in the fridge.

You might have egg and toast, or a glass of hot milk, or toasted cheese, but you feel your spirit crying out for something more.

Here is the answer: rösti. Rösti is a Swiss grated potato dish. In reality it is an excuse for eating a quarter of a pound of butter. While your loved one is taking a hot shower or mixing a drink, you can get to work.

Take off your coat and plunge one large Idaho potato into boiling water. By the time you have gotten into your pajamas and hung up your clothes, it is time to take it out—seven minutes, tops. This seems to stabilize the starch.

Gently heat a large quantity (half a stick) of unsalted butter in a skillet. It should foam but not turn brown. Grate the potato on the shredder side of the grater, press into a cake and slip into the butter. Fry till golden brown on both sides.

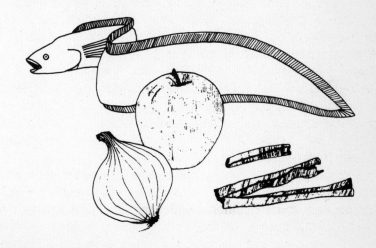

The result is somewhat indigestible, but after all, you have already been subjected to the truly indigestible. You will feel better for it. You and your companion—or you yourself (this recipe makes two big cakes: if you are alone, you can have both all to yourself)—will begin to see the evening's desecrations as an amusement.

Because you *are* the better for your horrible meal: fortified, uplifted and ready to face the myriad surprises and challenges in this most interesting and amazing of all possible worlds.

CHICKEN SALAD

C hicken salad has a certain glamour about it. Like the little black dress, it is chic and adaptable and can be taken anywhere. You can dress it down and feed it to a child, or dress it up and serve it at a dinner party. You can accessorize it in an interesting way and astonish your friends at lunch.

In the old days, chicken salad was served either to children, or at tearooms to ladies who had been shopping and wanted a light lunch. If you remember your Nancy Drew mysteries, you will recall that Nancy and her chums, wearing their sport frocks, would jump into Nancy's roadster and after chasing a nasty thief or smuggler, would stop at a tearoom and eat chicken salad and homemade rolls with iced tea. This old-fashioned chicken salad, which is composed of white meat of chicken, celery, a hint of onion and mayonnaise, is hard to find these days. It should come not as a crustless sandwich, but on a plate with a skinned tomato and some stuffed celery.

Fancy chicken salad has crowded the market, for we live in the age of the takeout gourmet shop. It is now possible to get chicken salad in styles previously unimagined (and often for good reason): with kiwi fruit and water chestnuts, blanched almonds, diced lemon and watercress, or prunes, mushrooms, black olives and pears.

Some of these are just as awful as the bland, unidentifiable stuff from the local deli, but some of them are inspired. I can never imagine exotic chicken salad being eaten by men, although they always seem to like it. Rather I envision a plate of chicken salad being presented to a beautifully dressed woman wearing a hat and a string of pearls. It can be said of chicken salad that it is stylish *and* ladylike.

I love chicken salad in its three incarnations: for children, for ladies' luncheons and for grown-up dinner parties. Needless to say, any of these can be happily eaten by anyone.

The child's chicken salad, best served on white toast, is the simple kind described before: chicken, onion, celery and mayonnaise.

The ladies' luncheon variety is what might be called New York Chicken Salad, in honor of the enormous varieties of chicken salad from the large number of fancy shops. My particular favorite sounds improbable but is extremely popular: chicken, pecans, golden raisins, chopped scallions and dill, bound with a curried mayonnaise. The mayonnaise doesn't have to be home-

made but homemade mayonnaise is always wonderful. The curry you must make yourself of one teaspoon each of ginger and turmeric, half a teaspoon of cumin, one quarter teaspoon of cinnamon and clove, and half a teaspoon of dried mustard and paprika—this is not an authentic curry but it is good.

For a grown-up dinner party I like a room-temperature chicken salad with funghi porcini. I have never been lucky enough to get my hands on any fresh funghi porcini, but dried will do. While the chicken breasts are poaching, the dried mushrooms are soaked in water. Then the mushroom liquor is strained through a coffee filter to remove the grit and set aside. The cooked chicken is cut into shreds and tossed with the mushrooms, olive oil, chopped scallion, salt, pepper and a teaspoon or so of the mushroom liquor. This makes a perfect summer dinner.

Then there is the perfect chicken salad, the salad that embodies the qualities to which all chicken salads aspire. It is an idealized version and its preparation might stand as a method for making all others:

PERFECT CHICKEN SALAD

serves 2-4

2 smallish chicken breasts
1 egg yolk
¾ cup light olive oil
¼ teaspoon dried mustard
1 small clove garlic, minced
pinch of salt
juice of ½ lemon
1 sprig fresh tarragon, finely chopped
2 scallions
thyme

1. First of all, the chicken breasts (bone in) must be poached very slowly and tenderly. The water must not boil but smile, as the French say, for an hour and a half or more. The result is chicken that is tender and almost custardy. It is never stringy or chewy. Save the broth.

2. The meat is skinned and taken off the bone and put into a bowl. Some of the broth is ladled over the meat. The bowl is covered and put into the refrigerator. The next day the meat is removed, the chicken jelly is scraped off and the meat is cut up. The chicken is moist and slightly gelatinous.

3. Then you make a mayonnaise of the egg yolk, olive oil, dried mustard, garlic, salt and enough lemon juice to thin it.

4. Add to this the tarragon, scallions and thyme—it is pointless to make this if you don't have fresh herbs. Pour over the cut-up chicken.

5. The result is ambrosial.

Now that you have made the chicken salad, what do you do with the stock left over from poaching the chicken breasts? You can freeze it, or use it as the base for almost any soup, or you can reward yourself for being the cook and make yourself the following treat:

LAST-MINUTE SOUP

for 1 person

one cup jellied stock, two asparagus chopped up,
some little pasta
one egg,
juice of half a lime,
and black pepper

Let the stock come to a simmer and add the asparagus and pasta: you can steal your child's pastina, or pasta stars. When the pasta has cooked, stir in a beaten egg and the lime juice. Add fresh black pepper and eat at once.

EASY COOKING
FOR EXHAUSTED PEOPLE

I am not a fancy cook or an ambitious one. I am a plain old cook. A while ago I was a person who liked to have friends over for dinner, and now that I have a child I am someone who is responsible for three meals a day plus snacks. And since I like to make things a little difficult for myself, I don't like the idea of my precious angel eating any old bread, so I bake my own.

Three meals a day seven days a week, even if you love to cook, is enough to get a person down, especially if the person has anything else to do such as pick a child up from school, write a novel, have time for such necessities as shopping, to say nothing of keeping up with friends and an occasional conversation with one's mate. Therefore it is smart to have under your belt a few really easy things that virtually cook themselves.

What you want is an enormous return on a small investment. Almost the only situation in which this is possible is cooking.

A long time ago I realized that every winter I developed an intense craving for boiled beef. I used to slake this desire at the

Ukrainian National Home restaurant, or at the old Lüchows, which made an admirable boiled beef and then cooled it to a jell and served it as *"Beef auf der Neuen Art."* It never occurred to me to make it myself, but of course it is one of the great easy things to make, as it cooks itself, presents interesting leftovers and can also be subsequently turned into soup.

I use a cut of meat called eye of chuck, a roundish loaf-shaped cut with almost no fat on it. It goes into a pot with three cloves of garlic, a sprig of rosemary (or not, if you don't like rosemary), some coarse black pepper and a couple of veal bones. What you really want is a calf's foot, but these are hard to find. The idea is to nourish the stock with all that rich veal gelatin. The meat is barely covered with spring or filtered water. You cover the pot and cook it in the oven at about 250° for three hours or so, until just tender. Then you add half a small green cabbage cut into wedges, a big carrot cut into chunks and a yellow onion, also cut into chunks. You can add turnips if you like them—I don't—and one large Idaho potato, peeled and cut into medium-size pieces. Cook for another hour or so, until the meat is very tender.

You can serve this the way the French do by serving the broth as the soup course, and then the meat and vegetables. Or you can serve it as the slobs do, and put everything into a big soup plate, and set the table with forks, knives and soup spoons. Some people like mustard, and some like horseradish, and some people, like me, like very hot Indian lime pickle which goes nicely with boiled beef.

If you have any broth left over, you can use it for soup stock, or you can poach some lentils in it, slice up the leftover meat and have lentil and beef salad for lunch. Or you can slice up whatever meat is left over and make sandwiches, or cut it into strips and marinate it in a little olive oil, red pepper flakes, scallions and lemon juice. Served with sliced cucumbers and leftover rice this makes a tasty dish.

If you are a vegetarian, or run with vegetarians, a delicious, almost work-free dish is a vegetarian chili. It is not authentic but it is good.

Until recently the very idea of vegetarian chili made me queasy. Awful recipes for it abound in health-oriented cookbooks. This summer, at a little family-run restaurant called Chelsea in Great Barrington, Massachusetts, I tasted vegetarian chili for the first time and found it delicious. The trick, the owner told me, was to use four kinds of beans.

At home, I set to work. I used small red beans (kidney beans are too coarse for this dish), aduki beans (tiny little red beans from the health food store), black beans and urad dal—tiny black lentils you can find at the Indian store.

On the bottom of a kettle put a bay leaf. Then wash one cup of black beans, one cup of little red beans and half a cup each of aduki beans and urad dal. Needless to say, these proportions are flexible. This will feed three or four people. Put the beans in the pot and cover with the cut-up contents and the juice of a large can of Italian plum tomatoes, three cloves of garlic chopped, one chopped onion and one large medium dried chili (available in Mexican or Spanish groceries), washed and seeded. Add chili powder to taste, and water if necessary. Put the pot on the stove at the merest simmer and leave all day, stirring from time to time. The beans need not be soaked. As Buster Holmes, owner of Buster Holmes's Restaurant in New Orleans, points out, beans don't get mushy unless you soak them first.

Before serving you can stir in a little olive oil, to make them creamy. Or not. Serve with rice or cornbread.

Now you have two extremely easy main dishes. A salad is of course the product of a few seconds' work. But what for dessert?

In his memoir *In My Father's Court*, Isaac Bashevis Singer mentions his mother's baked pears—long baked with a scrap of vanilla and cinnamon, and a curl of lemon peel. For these pears I use a tagine pot my cousin brought me from Morocco—a dish of medium depth with a conical top, both earthenware. While I have never made a tagine—Moroccan stew—I have baked apples and pears with great success in my tagine. Any earthenware dish with a cover will work as well.

Set whole Seckel pears in an earthenware dish, sprinkle with sugar (or vanilla sugar—sugar that sits around with a vanilla bean in the middle). Put in one-half cup of water, one cinnamon stick and one curlicue of lemon peel. Cover and bake at 300° for one and a half hours.

And, unless you want to live on cold cereal, there's nothing easier than that.

HOW TO GIVE A PARTY

I have never thought of myself as much of a party-giver, but it turns out I have given my share over the years.

By "party" I mean a gathering of more than eight whose eventual destination is not the dining room table: in short, there are parties, and there are dinner parties. And while I know there are such things as large parties which feature an evening meal, in my household this is called "having people over for dinner" and the number, except for Christmas Eve or Thanksgiving, is usually six or under.

A party by its nature is free-floating. People are free to float about your rooms grinding cake crumbs into your rugs, scattering cigarette ash on your wood floors, scaring your cat and leaving their glasses to make rings on your furniture. This sort of thing is enthralling to some potential hosts and hostesses, horrific to others. Most people feel a combination of these things: the idea of a party fills them half with horror, half with excitement.

But no matter how you dread them, parties must be given because events must be celebrated: birthdays, book publications, engagements, homecomings and so on. Birthdays, especially, come year after year and one must know what to do about them. Those of us who have no servants like to keep things simple and still show people a good time. This is easier to do than one might think.

The first thing is to figure out what sort of party you like, and what sort of party you like to give. After years of contemplation (and the arrival of a baby who is now a child), I realize that I do not like parties at night: I am too tired. I do not want to feed and bathe a child and then feed sixteen adults, or spend what might be perfectly useful time asleep cleaning up. After nine o'clock I begin to wilt, and I notice that others do, too. My favorite party is a tea party. These days I like one that begins at three and ends around five thirty.

A tea party is suitable for people of all ages. It comes at a time of day when people often have time on their hands or are feeling inclined toward a little something to eat and drink and someone to talk to. A tea party accommodates your grown-up friends with and without children, and it accommodates the children, too. As all parents know, at four o'clock, children must be fed something.

At four in the afternoon, everyone feels a little peckish but only the British have institutionalized this feeling. Every year one English magazine or another carries an article about the decline of the tearoom, but teatime still exists and many tea shops serve it. It is a perfect child meal since children and their caregivers tend to droop around four o'clock and need to be revived.

There are two kinds of tea: high and low. In this country high tea is mistakenly construed to mean an elaborate tea with lots of cakes and cookies. The fact is that high tea is merely a dinner tea, that is, tea served at six o'clock with a light evening meal, for instance, poached eggs on toast, or, as I was once served in a hotel in Brecon, Wales, a bowl of something called Windsor (or brown) soup, and a mutton chop with bristles on it, and a big cup of tea.

Low tea, taken at four, may be as humble as bread and butter and a pot of tea with a plate of biscuits, or it may be as elaborate as a large iced cake, a plate of strawberries and a heap of tea sandwiches. For inspiration, it is useful to read *Mary Poppins* by P. L. Travers or the early novels of Iris Murdoch, in which tea menus are elaborately described.

The great advantage of a tea party is that everything can be done in advance and the hostess gets to put her feet up and sit around for a little while before the thundering herds appear. Furthermore, the menu should resemble a crazy quilt or set of unmatched china. The chocolate cake sits next to the cheese buns, and the cucumber and anchovy sandwiches commingle with the shortbread. In short, you can serve four or five (or two or three) of your favorite things and a pot of tea (with coffee or wine for those who do not drink tea).

There are times when the tea party will not do: Christmas Eve and the Fourth of July. Christmas Eve requires a sit-down dinner with a big bird or large fish. Our Christmas Eve menu is not fixed. One year we had goose, a magnificent-looking creature sitting majestically on a huge platter. When this enormous bird was carved, each person received a wisp of meat, since that is about all you get from a goose, and my husband had an allergic reaction to it and had to be put to bed with two Benadryl tablets. We have had capon, ducks, turkey and last year we had salmon which was enjoyed by all except for one of the guests who confessed at the table to being highly allergic to fish.

A festival meal requires one big item, some elegant side dishes and a wonderful dessert. Then everyone leaves the table and sits in the living room drinking decaffeinated espresso, eating pistachio nuts, oranges and chocolates, leaving your floor littered with pistachio shells and little shreds of the colored paper from the chocolates.

The Fourth of July was always taken seriously in my family when I was a child, and I have maintained this tradition. Each year the menu is always the same: fried chicken, potato salad and cole slaw, with something down home for dessert: peaches and ice cream or gingerbread.

But when birthdays come around, I always revert to the tea party. This began with a tea party to celebrate my husband's birthday. It was neither high nor low, but a combination. Twenty-five people consumed a large platter of ham sandwiches, another of cucumber sandwiches, a tower of brownies, a ginger cake, an enormous Latvian birthday cake (a coffee cake made of saffron-flavored yeast dough spiked with yellow raisins and formed in the shape of a figure eight), a basket of cheese straws, two pots of baked beans, a basin of strawberries and a samovar of tea.

ELZA JURJEVICS' LATVIAN BIRTHDAY CAKE

1 stick butter
1¼ cup milk
1 tablespoon saffron
3 tablespoons water
4 cups flour
½ cup sugar
1 tablespoon yeast
1 medium potato, boiled
1 cup raisins
4 ounces sour cream
1 egg beaten with a little water
sugar

This is a saffron-flavored coffee cake that can also be made into wreaths or buns. The traditional shape for a birthday cake is a figure eight.

1. Butter a baking sheet and set aside. Preheat oven to 350°. Melt butter in milk and set aside.
2. Boil saffron in water and set aside.

3. Sift flour, sugar and yeast. Sieve in potato, while hot, and mix it into the flour with your fingers. Add raisins.

4. Add butter and milk to the flour. Add the saffron. Beat in sour cream and then beat until glossy. You do not knead this dough. Let the dough rise until doubled in bulk.

5. Beat it down and, adding a little flour to make the dough less sticky, beat it again. Then form the dough into a long roll by rolling and stretching gently. Place on the buttered baking sheet in the shape of a figure eight—you are aiming for something that looks like a big pretzel.

6. Butter two custard cups and place them in the open parts of the pretzel to keep them open during baking. Brush the top with an egg wash, scatter with sugar and bake at 350° for forty-five minutes.

This cake is served with the candles, in little candle holders, in the openings.

This is really a coffee cake with saffron dough. The dough can be formed into delicious little buns instead of a figure eight. My mother-in-law makes hers the size of coat buttons, and in my house dozens of them vanish in an instant. They are known as yellow bread, and I have noticed that our cat is crazy about them too.

The dough is a beautiful, rich yellow. The saffron gives it a subtle, exotic and quite indescribable taste. This is not meant to be a very sweet cake. It is eaten plain or with butter and jam, and it keeps well if you are lucky enough to have any left.

Each year our daughter's guest list gets a little longer but the party stays the same: tea sandwiches, a small Latvian birthday cake (since she is half-Latvian) and her two personal choices, a carrot cake made from a recipe in *Jewish Cooking* and made-leines, half in the traditional shape and half in the shape of a scallop shell. To use up the egg whites, a plate of chocolate meringues. Tea and coffee for the grown-ups, juice and milk for the children. This party begins at three and ends at five, before there is time to get overtired, cranky or upset. Birthday parties are often more of a strain on young children than many adults realize, and it seems a good idea to keep them fairly simple. The rule is that if the adults are having a nice, relaxed time, the children will, too, and many small children will stand by the table amusing themselves nicely by picking all the cucumbers off the cucumber sandwiches. Because a tea party does not rely merely on cake and ice cream, children do not fill up on sugar and if the party ends at five, you have an hour to unwind before dinner.

My birthday is a sort of makeshift affair. My favorite cake is gingerbread with chocolate icing, and I make the cake the night before. Sometimes I make two layers, and sometimes I split one. When the cake is cool, I spread the middle with a very, very thick layer of raspberry jam and stick the layers together. The top is spread with a thin layer of jam and the cake is left to stand, uniced, overnight. The next morning I make a plain butter, sugar and chocolate icing—any standard cookbook will give a recipe with proportions, or see page 172—on which, at my daughter's insistence, sprinkles of various kinds—chocolate and multi-colored—are festooned.

This year to go with the cake I made a plate of cheese buns—white bread dough rolled thin, stuffed with Gruyère, chopped scallions, black pepper and a little olive oil, scattered with chopped rosemary and baked in the oven.

The guests included two girls, seven and eight, a nine-year-old boy, two three-year-old girls (one mine, one my oldest friend's) and two baby boys, aged seven months and ten months, plus various parents.

"Don't give the baby any birthday cake," said the mother of the ten-month-old baby. "It's too spicy. It will make him cry."

"It's my birthday," I said. "Can't he have a taste?"

"Just icing," said his mother.

The icing was a huge success.

"Oh, give him a little cake," said his father.

"No!" said his mother. "It will make him scream."

I gave the baby a little piece of icing with cake attached. He began to laugh and pound his fist, which means "More!"

The babies all ate ginger cake. The three-year-olds ate cake and then attempted to pick off all the icing. The older children ate cake and cheese buns and then everyone helped clean up. By the time the last dish had been put in the dishwasher, the three-year-olds had been fed their suppers and given their baths. One was asleep in her bed and the other was in a taxi on her way to *her* bed. Every crumb had been eaten, the table had been wiped. The toys had been put away and there was a relative degree of order in the house. It was seven thirty, with plenty of time to finish the paper, read a book and send out for Chinese food.

Now, that's what I call a good party.

HOW TO MAKE GINGERBREAD

G ingerbread, that most evocative of nursery treats, has gone out of fashion and even the revival in American cooking has failed to bring it back. You never see it on menus or in bakeries, except in the form of gingerbread cookie men at Christmastime.

I love gingerbread in its true cake form—moist, spongy and spicy. It is strictly home food, but no one makes it anymore. Those who crave it get their fix from mixes, and if you give them the real thing, they appear confused. Why doesn't *their* gingerbread taste that good? There is nothing to be said about mixes: they are uniformly disgusting. Besides, gingerbread made from scratch takes very little time and gives back tenfold what you put into it. Baking gingerbread perfumes a house as nothing else. It is good eaten warm or cool, iced or plain. It improves with age, should you be lucky or restrained enough to keep any around.

Gingerbread exists in some form or other all throughout northern Europe. Florence White's classic *Good Things in England*, for example, has twelve recipes. Mrs. Mary Randolph's *The Virginia Housewife*, published in 1824, has three. It is definitely food for a cold climate. Its spicy, embracing taste is the perfect thing for a winter afternoon. Ginger warms up your stomach (and is believed by many to purify the blood). When you serve it, once they have stopped giving you a funny look, people often say: "Gingerbread! I haven't had that since I was a child."

If you are feeding sophisticates, you can either take them back to childhood and serve it plain with a little whipped cream, or fancy it up by adding crème fraîche and a poached Seckel pear (page 161).

I have tried any number of recipes and have finally found the one I like best. Its basic proportions come from a recipe for Tropical Gingerbread in a spiral-bound book entitled *The Charleston Receipts.* This gem, which has been published since 1950 by the Junior League of Charleston (and is still available for ten dollars by writing to The Charleston Receipts, Box 177, Charleston, South Carolina 29402), contains wonderful recipes for everything from Brunswick stew to scones to shorten' bread and spoonbread. Tropical Gingerbread, however, calls for coconut which I feel has no place in gingerbread at all, so I have felt free to make a few changes and additions to an otherwise excellent recipe.

Instead of the white sugar called for, I use either light or dark brown. Light brown makes a slightly spongier cake, and dark brown creates a more sugary crust. I also add two teaspoons of lemon brandy, a heavenly elixir easily homemade by taking the peel from two lemons, cutting very close to get mostly zest, beating up the peels to release the oils and steeping them in four ounces of decent brandy. I have had my bottle for thirteen years and have replenished the brandy many times.

Besides the ginger, the heart of gingerbread is molasses. Now, there is molasses and molasses and there is the King of Molasses, which is available in the South but virtually unknown in the North. It comes in a bright yellow can and can be ordered by mail. In black letters is the following message:

STEEN'S
PURE RIBBON CANE SYRUP
(A delicious table syrup—soppin' good)

"Non sulphur or lime"
Rich in available iron
Made and put up by
THE C.S. STEEN SYRUP MILL, INC.
ABBEVILLE, LOUISIANA 70510
Nothing added—Nothing Extracted—Open Kettle

I was once given a tin by a Cajun friend, and when I ran out, I called the Steen Company and asked how to get more. A case of four twenty-five-ounce tins now costs $15.49 with shipping. On the back of the tin is their recipe for gingerbread which is very delicious but extremely sticky and you must therefore eat it with a fork. I like mine much less sticky so you can eat it with your hands. You do not need Steen's to make gingerbread, but I see it as one of life's greatest delights: a cheap luxury.

The following recipe makes one nine-inch cake:

GINGERBREAD CAKE

1 stick sweet butter
½ cup light or dark brown sugar .
½ cup molasses
2 eggs
1½ cups flour
½ teaspoon baking soda
1 generous tablespoon ground ginger
1 teaspoon cinnamon
¼ teaspoon ground cloves
¼ teaspoon ground allspice
2 teaspoons lemon brandy, or plain vanilla extract
½ cup buttermilk (or milk with a little yogurt beaten into it)

1. Butter a 9-inch cake tin and set aside. Preheat oven to 350°.
2. Cream butter with brown sugar. Beat until fluffy and add molasses.

3. Beat in eggs.

4. Add flour, baking soda and ground ginger (this can be adjusted to taste, but I like it very gingery). Add cinnamon, cloves and allspice.

5. Add lemon brandy or plain vanilla extract. Lemon extract will not do. *Then add buttermilk (or milk-yogurt mixture) and turn batter into the buttered tin.*

6. Bake at 350° for between twenty and thirty minutes (check after twenty minutes have passed). Test with a broom straw, and cool on a rack.

Recently my daughter came into a set of child-sized baking things—a roaster big enough for a pear, a tiny double boiler, a finger-sized eggbeater plus two little muffin tins and three saucer-sized cake pans. One afternoon, I decided to bake the gingerbread in these pans.

The muffins came out the size of coat buttons and the cakes were six inches in diameter. As I looked at those little cakes, I realized I had stumbled into something Big.

I fed the muffins to my daughter and her friends as I hatched my plans for the cakes. I would make a three-layer ginger cake, each layer spread with seedless raspberry jam and covered with chocolate icing. I got out my dime store cake-decorating kit and then made the icing. I intended to decorate this cake with swags and garlands but I struck too fast. The cake had not quite cooled and my swirls slid down the sides and melted. The result was not a thing of beauty but it didn't last very long, either.

CHOCOLATE ICING

½ stick sweet butter
4 tablespoons unsweetened cocoa
1 teaspoon vanilla brandy, or vanilla extract or plain brandy
1 cup powdered sugar

❊

1. Cream butter. When fluffy add unsweetened cocoa.

2. If you have some, add vanilla brandy (easily made by steeping a couple of cut-up vanilla beans in brandy—another excellent thing to have around), or plain vanilla extract or plain brandy. Then add powdered sugar, a little at a time until you get the consistency you want.

This cake is also delicious with lemon icing. Substitute for the cocoa the zest of one big lemon, one teaspoon of lemon brandy (or extract) and one tablespoon of lemon juice, and proceed as in chocolate icing.

Lemon icing, I have discovered, must stand around for a while in order to bloom. At first taste, it is impossibly sweet but after an hour or so it mellows into something suave and buttery.

Of course, you need not ice gingerbread at all. You can bake it in an adult-sized pan and shake powdered sugar on top or serve it with ice cream or leave it alone. Cut into wedges, it goes a long way, unlike the three-decker child cake.

This little three-layer cake will feed six delicate, well-mannered people with small appetites who are on diets and have just had a large meal, or four fairly well-mannered people who are not terribly hungry. Two absolute pigs can devour it in one sitting—half for you and half for me—with a glass of milk and a cup of coffee and leave not a crumb for anyone else.

STUFFED BREAST OF VEAL: A BAD IDEA

There comes a time in every cook's life when he or she feels he or she ought to make a stuffed breast of veal. I know this impulse well, for I have fallen prey to it.

Like many others, I too went to the butcher in advance. I asked him to bone the breast of veal and save the bones for me. I went home and consulted a number of cookbooks until I found what I felt would be a magnificent stuffing—rice, spinach, parsley, garlic, ham, grated cheese and pine nuts, or something like that. I got my meat from the butcher and made veal stock from the bones. I stuffed that critter, stitched it up and basted it with butter and stock. I watched it tenderly.

When it was cooked, I sliced it and fed it to friends. It looked very impressive on its platter and after all that work it tasted all right but nothing at all to rave about. The next day I ran the leftovers through a meat grinder and made some nice enough croquettes.

I once gave in to the impulse to bone a chicken and stuff it with pâté. This was in my younger days when that sort of thing seemed like a good idea. Triple bypass surgery on the vice-presidents of a medium-sized corporation could have been performed in the time it took me to bone this chicken because the trick was to bone it without cutting into it. You sort of wiggled the knife inside the cavity and got the bones from underneath. When I had finished, I was exhausted and the poor little chicken looked like a dead basketball. But nevertheless, I was determined to stuff that creature with a fancy mixture of ham, chicken, pistachio nuts, cream, cognac and so forth. It makes me shudder to think of it.

I roasted it in the oven and I felt it smelled peculiar. Not off, or high—just odd. The pâté canceled out the roasting chicken smell and vice versa. When it was cooked I left it to sit a little and collect itself and then I sliced it. It, too, looked very impressive and it didn't taste bad, but no one really liked it very much. It was confusing: was this a chicken or a pâté? In restaurants people expect this sort of thing. In other people's houses, it seems, they do not. They like to have a nice straightforward meal: one thing or another, *but not both*. That is the great virtue of people's houses over restaurants. And when you are bored with home cooking, it is the great glory of restaurants (unless you are in one of those exhausted states in which you want something that tastes like something you would cook but you don't want to cook it) to provide you with something thrilling.

I have made homemade pretzels, a very good idea, and lemon-flavored babas, a not so good idea. After all, the joy of cooking is the joy of discovery.

Not very long ago I decided to buy a pheasant. I found one at my farmers' market and had a chat with the pheasant farmer.

"Has this bird been hung?" I said, remembering from English cookbooks that you are supposed to roast a pheasant when its tail feathers fall off. English friends often claim they like pheasant so high that you can mash it with a fork. I did not think I could get my husband and two-and-a-half-year-old daughter to eat something that had rotted out its feathers, so I felt I needed information.

"It is not permitted by law to sell a hung pheasant," the farmer said. "I like 'em hung a little when I keep them for myself, but we have to sell them fresh." He produced for me a naked carcass in a plastic bag. No feathers of any sort in sight.

"What does it taste like?" I said.

"Chicken," the farmer said. "A little tastier. Not too much meat on it, though."

Why am I buying this? I wondered as I took it home. I roasted it in a casserole and served it for Saturday night supper. We all agreed that it tasted like very expensive chicken and until I get my hands on one that has had a little time to accumulate a little more taste, I am not going to buy pheasant again.

On the other hand, I was once given a pasta machine and instantly set about making pasta. My pasta was not beautiful and it did not emerge from its final rolling in one long, beautiful sheet, but it certainly was delicious and not overly time-consuming. I have also made spinach gnocchi, a messy job which takes a fair amount of time and pays you back a thousandfold.

For years I have been cruising past the zucchini blossoms during the summer at my greenmarket and not buying them. This year, I gave in. The blossoms were attached to tiny little zucchinis, the sort beloved by my daughter who likes a baby vegetable. I took them home, snipped them off, and turned to my Italian cookbooks to see what to do with them.

All agreed that I should dip them in batter and fry them in oil. No one agreed how the batter should be made. One recipe called for one egg, one cup of flour, one tablespoon of lemon juice and one of water. This looked as if it would produce plaster of Paris, and so I cut it down to one-fourth cup flour, and a little more water. I dipped the zucchini blossoms in the batter and fried them in olive oil. They puffed up beautifully and turned golden brown. I had no idea what they would taste like.

At the dining room table, my husband and daughter waited patiently. At last a little platter of these blossoms was placed before them. I did not know what to expect, but I have come to believe that the exotic will often let you down, especially if you have never tasted what it is supposed to be like.

I now feel that the real purpose of zucchini is to produce zucchini blossoms, and that anyone with a small child should think seriously about laying in a good supply in June. No sooner had this platter been placed before us than its contents disappeared.

"More zucchini flowers!" my daughter howled, but it was too late. We had eaten them all.

Of course there is a motto here: always try everything even if it turns out to be a dud. We learn by doing. If you never stuff a chicken with pâté, you will never know that it is an unwise thing to do, and if you never buy zucchini flowers you will never know that you are missing one of the glories of life.

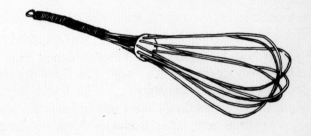

BLACK CAKE

When my daughter was a year old, she acquired a baby-sitter from the island of St. Vincent named Betty Chambers, who came to play with her three mornings a week. Shortly thereafter I became acquainted with something called Black Cake, a traditional West Indian fruitcake served at weddings, Christmas and other festivities. One morning Betty appeared with an odd-looking slice of something that might have been tar with elaborate white frosting on the top.

"What is this?" I said.

"Black Cake," Betty said. "I thought you might like to taste it."

I took a tentative bite and was transported into a state of rapture and admiration.

There is fruitcake, and there is Black Cake, which is to fruitcake what the Brahms piano quartets are to Muzak. Its closest relatives are plum pudding and black bun, but it leaves both in the dust. Black Cake, like truffles and vintage Burgundy, is deep, complicated and intense. It has taste and aftertaste. It demands to be eaten in a slow, meditative way. The texture is complicated, too—dense and light at the same time.

"How did you make this?" I gasped.

"Oh, it's simple," said Betty. "You just chop up all the fruits and marinate them for six months in a bottle of Passover wine and a bottle of dark rum."

This sounded not only daunting but disappointing since there was only a tiny scrap of the slice left and I was forced to share it with my child, who said "More!" in a loud voice.

I grabbed a pencil, sat Betty down and got the recipe. It is a beautiful, old-fashioned recipe which was handed down to Betty by her mother, who got it from her mother, and so on. It comes from a time when cakes were cakes and no one bothered much about using a dozen eggs at a shot.

It is not necessary to marinate the fruit for six months, although serious West Indian bakers always have fruit ready. Betty starts her fruit a month to two weeks before baking.

A Black Cake really *is* black, not dark brown. It gets its blackness in part from burnt sugar essence, which is available in West Indian grocery stores. If it's unavailable, Betty suggests putting a pound of brown sugar in a heavy skillet with a little water and boiling it gently until it begins to turn black. You do not want to overboil. It should be only slightly bitter, black and definitely burnt.

This recipe makes two deep nine-inch cakes.

BLACK CAKE PART I:
THE FRUIT

1 pound raisins
1 pound prunes
1 pound currants
1 pound glacé cherries
¾ pound mixed peel
1 bottle Passover wine
1 bottle dark rum (750 ml.)

1. Chop raisins, prunes, currants, glacé cherries and ¾ pound of

mixed peel extra, extra fine. For a grainier texture, leave some of the currants whole. Pour into a large bowl or crock and cover with Passover wine and one bottle of the darkest rum you can find. Marinate at least two weeks—but the longer the better—up to six months.

BLACK CAKE PART II:
BAKING

1 pound butter
1 pound dark brown sugar
1 tablespoon vanilla extract
½ teaspoon nutmeg
½ teaspoon cinnamon
1 dozen eggs
1 pound plus ½ cup flour
3 teaspoons baking powder
1 pound burnt sugar, or 4 ounces burnt sugar essence

1. Butter and flour two deep 9-inch cake tins and set aside. Preheat oven to 350°.

2. Cream butter and brown sugar.

3. Add the fruit and wine.

4. Add vanilla, nutmeg and cinnamon.

5. Beat in eggs.

6. Add flour and baking powder, burnt sugar or burnt sugar essence if you can find it. Batter should be dark brown.

7. Bake in cake tins for 1 to 1¼ hours at 350°.

When the cake is absolutely cool, wrap it in waxed paper or tin-foil—not plastic wrap—and let it sit until you are ready to ice it.

BLACK CAKE PART III:
THE ICING

Black Cake must be iced. The icing is the simplest white icing made of powdered sugar and egg white with the addition of half a teaspoon of almond extract. This is essential and a perfect foil to the complexity of the cake. Since Black Cakes are often wedding cakes, it is traditional to decorate them: colored icing, flowers, swags and garlands. Any standard cookbook has a recipe for white icing and the decoration is up to the cook.

I confess that I have not yet baked my Black Cake. I am waiting. Last Christmas Betty gave us one as a present, and it was polished off on Christmas Eve by ten adults and two children under three. But when I brought it to the table I was greeted with considerable skepticism.

The same people more or less come to Christmas Eve dinner every year. The year before I had decided that I would bake a Dundee Cake (a fruitcake heavy on the candied cherries) from a recipe in a British magazine. This was a terrible mistake.

Our guests were presented with a ring of buttered sawdust in which was embedded a series of jujubes (for those who have never seen them, these are little fruit candies with the consistency of hard, congealed rubber cement).

Therefore when I appeared with Betty's Black Cake (on the top of which I had placed a sprig of holly), I was not greeted with jubilant shouts.

"What's that?" said our friend Seymour, victim of last Christmas's Dundee Cake.

"This is an authentic Black Cake," I said. "It is made with St. Vincent rum."

No one looked very thrilled except my daughter, who had been talking about Black Cake for a couple of weeks.

I cut into it and took out a slice.

"By God!" said Seymour. "It *is* black!"

I cut each person a small slice. Black Cake is, after all, very rich, and besides, I wanted leftovers. A total silence ensued, which is either a good or a bad sign.

In this case it was a good sign for our guests and a bad sign for me, since I was counting on having some Black Cake around for a week or so to nibble on in the afternoon. The two children under three each ate a considerable portion but since the alcohol had all been baked out it did not have the soporific effect the adults were hoping for. Black Cake is *bracing*.

This is an easy recipe to cut in half, but it seems a shame to do it. The spirit of this recipe is celebratory, lavish and open-handed. It seems the right thing to make two and give one to someone you feel very strongly about.

Fruitcakes abound in the Caribbean. I have had a couple—a dark fruitcake from Jamaica and one from Barbados. Both were full of heavy fruit and raw rum. But Black Cake! Black Cake is in a class by itself. I have never had anything like it before or since, and it is *not* an acquired taste.

One bite is all it takes.

INDEX